CAFES

& COFFEE SHOPS

CAFES

& COFFEE SHOPS

Edited by Martin M. Pegler, SVM

McGRAW-HILL, INC.

New York   San Francisco   Washington, D.C.   Auckland   Bogotá
Caracas   Lisbon   London   Madrid   Mexico City   Milan
Montreal   New Delhi   San Juan   Singapore
Sydney   Tokyo   Toronto

Retail Reporting Corporation
302 Fifth Avenue
New York, NY 10001

Distributors to the trade in the United States and Canada
McGraw-Hill, Inc
1221 Avenue of the Americas
New York, NY 10020

Distributors outside the United States and Canada
Hearst Books International
1350 Avenue of the Americas
New York, NY 10019

Library of Congress Cataloging in Publication Data:
Cafes & Coffee Shops

Printed in Hong Kong
ISBN 0-07-049393-6
Second Printing 1996
Designed by Bernard Schleifer

CONTENTS

INTRODUCTION

White dinner cloths, wafer-thin china, classic silver and delicate crystal stemware are out. Pewter, ceramics, pottery, wood, bright patterns and colors are in. Long dinner dresses, white opera gloves, tux and white ties are out. Sportswear, sports jackets, casual wear, and shoes with or without socks are in.

Dining out today is rarely a formal occasion of gentle conversation and soft background music; more likely it is an event—a celebration—like a barbecue or picnic brought indoors—the 4th of July with or without fireworks. The world has become a more casual and relaxed place—more uninhibited and eating out is more than taking sustenance—it is another reason for having fun. The string quartet is rarely heard and the show tunes of Muzak are passe. Today, more and more diners are trying to be heard over the throbbing sound of heavy metal or the unrelenting drive of Dixieland jazz. The young man and woman—out on a date of discovery—more often than not will only have eyes for the theatrical exhibition of flamboyant chefs preparing flambeed desserts or watching swirling, high-flying pizzas making the rounds, the workings in the world of wok-ery or the carousel of roasted meats and chickens rotating over the charcoal grills or in rotary rotisseries. Dining out is another form of entertainment and this entertainment appeals to the senses of smell, sight, touch, hearing—and, of course, taste.

Along with the relaxed attitude towards dining goes an even more relaxing attitude towards "the coffee break." The "break" has broken out of the office and people are rediscovering the pleasures of the social cup of coffee, tea or chocolate—plus a tasty baked tidbit or bisquit in a setting that can be old, worn, and as mismatched as a thrift shop—or crisp and contemporary as a Milanese design—or as high tech as an atomic submarine. Coffee house and coffee shops are also purveyors of blends of exotic coffees, tea and such white customers can sample and then buy to savor at home. Wine bars seem to have gone the way of Muzak and now Brew Houses are the "in" places for the young, the informal and the casual lifestyles of today.

"Food: Retail Design & Display" is gone. In its place and in keeping with the new trends, is the new title, "Cafes & Coffee Houses." This edition focuses on the excitement, color, and the themes found in casual dining establishments. It also includes what is happening in markets, specialty stores and fast food operations in and out of food courts. Theater and spectacle are all part of the presentation and merchandising of the product. Our examples literally from around the world and include examples from Europe and Latin America.

No matter what your political affiliation or your religious preference—we call all take these familiar words which appear in The New Testament as our credo:

"Take thine ease; eat, drink and be merry."

This is what dining is all about today.

MARTIN M. PEGLER

CAFES
& COFFEE SHOPS

COFFEE SHOPS
& COFFEE HOUSES,
TEA SALONS,
CAFES &
CAFETERIAS

T SALON

CELLAR, GUGGENHEIM MUSEUM

SOHO, NEW YORK, NY

In Soho where coffee bars would be as natural as breathing, it is T Salon in the basement of the Guggenheim Salon on Prince and Mercer streets that has people lining up to taste and buy tea—the coffee alternative. Though this chapter is all about coffee—coffee shops, coffee houses, cafes and such—we open with one of the newest and most successful ventures in purveying "relaxing brews."

Miriam Novalle, the owner of the 5,000 sq. ft. tea room/tea emporium, sees tea coming in as a new, strong taste satisfier that has no social or ethnic boundaries. It isn't just the stereotyped, blue rinsed, white haired ladies in gloves sipping tea—or the ultra social quality of "high tea" which is becoming popular in some of the better hotels in the U.S.; tea is for everybody. On a Saturday it is not unusual for T to cater to over 1,000 tea drinkers enjoying any one of the 20 different brews of tea or purchasing some of the 280 different teas available in the shop.

The designers of T, L. Bogdanow & Associates, chose to leave some of the space in its original state in this landmarked old building.

It is "the contrast that makes the room more interesting and authentic." The stripped, cast iron columns, the arched brick walls, and the glass block sidewalk vaults are all "Soho architectural elements." Winding around the columns is the 70 ft. long bar made of 2" thick curly maple wood with a copper face. Beautifully detailed— "it is both contemporary and elegant." The bar is the visual centerpiece of the sprawling space which includes antique furniture, custom light fixtures, and various flooring surfaces.

Upon entering T, the visitor may opt for the cocktail bar on the left—turn to the right and take in the many splendors, sights and smells of tea, teapots and tea paraphernalia in the open emporium— or go straight on to either the juice bar or the dining room beyond.

The assorted, mismatched but definitely on-target furniture was purchased by Ms. Novalle in England and includes old hardware cabinets, antique tables and glass front display cabinets. The designers provided unifying and atmospheric elements and materials like solid cherry wood flooring, slate tiles, a full commercial kitchen and the aforementioned bar which is "a sculptural reference, perhaps, to the 20th century art upstairs."

There are two entrances to T: one is from the museum and the other is from the street corner of Prince & Mercer.

DESIGN: *L. Bogdanow & Associates, Architects, New York, NY*
Larry Bogdanow, Warren Ashworth, Kate Webb

CHOCK FULL O'NUTS

Welcome back—welcome to the return of the shop with the "Heavenly Coffee." Before all the rage of the Seattle and Vancouver coffee houses—way back even before W.W.II, there was a Chock Full O'Nuts; a coffee vending store with more than just coffee to serve. The company, whose outlets had almost all disappeared, is like "Dolly"—back where she belongs. As the firm says—"the tradition brews on."

This new prototype design by Eric N. Singer & Associates is dramatic and sophisticated but it also makes a refreshing re-entry for the venerable coffee packager with a contemporary look that is "friendly and inviting to all." The management of Chock Full O'Nuts says, "First we entice customers with the aroma of fresh roasted coffee, the sound of brewing high quality cappuccino, espresso-based specialty drinks and the premium beverages; and the warm, cozy 'sit awhile' atmosphere of a coffee bar." Then they offer quality sandwiches, light meals and home-baked snacks at reasonable prices.

The store has three levels of 1,500 sq. ft. each. The basement is where the kitchen is located. The store front is designed to "open up." The glass panels can slide back into a concealed closet and thus create a "sidewalk cafe" in an area that actually prohibits the use of the sidewalk for dining. Patrons are inside but feel as though they are outside. On the main level, the coffee/espresso bar is on the right while the wall of food/food bar is located towards the rear of the space. A stairway connects to the second level and the dining room there. The opening above the coffee/espresso bar allows the aromas and sounds of brewing coffee to permeate the upper level.

DESIGN: *Eric N. Singer & Associates, Eric Singer, AIA*
PHOTOGRAPHER: *Jason Schmidt Photographer*

Cherrywood, custom stained to the designer's specification, is used for the millwork, cabinetry, the seating, and also for the menuboards which incorporate the company's long familiar checkerboard logo design. Black granite counter tops have the yellow and black checkerboard incorporated into the customer-facing, front edges. The floors and base board are covered with porcelain ceramic tiles and an eggshell paint is used on the drywall constructed walls.

With the return of the popularity of "coffee houses" and after a hiatus of two decades, Chock Full O'Nuts is back and the new prototype design opened on the same Madison Ave. corner where many years ago another Chock Full O'Nuts stood. It is a welcome return the many new diners are finding out about the famous nutted cream cheese sandwiches on raisin bread that the "old times" fondly remember and are glad to be able to order again. A whole new generation is now sampling this staple from the '40s, '50s and '60s. Retro lives!

LA VENEZIA

For many years the rich green facade accented in gold and highlighted with green and white striped awnings has been the mecca for coffee lovers lost in malls across the country. They followed their noses till their eyes spotted the traditional Barnie's shop front where they knew salvation was at hand. Barnie's has now ventured out with a new format and a new name—a free standing cafe and coffee house: this is La Venezia.

The new operation has borrowed liberally from the design elements that have proven such effective signature notes in the Barnie's stores. Rich cream colored marble tones are combined with the handsome cherry wood used on the bar in the coffee area as well as for the wine/liquor bar. As accents, the designers selected the jewel tones that are used on the Barnie's packaging: amethyst plum, sapphire blue and emerald green. What is especially noteworthy are the fabulous Tiffany windows which are on loan from the Charles Hosmer Morse Foundation. They include the peacock window, the grape arbor window and three panels from the classic Brown Renfrew Mansion in New Castle, PA. Also used in the design of the cafe are green windows which were originally used in a church in Brooklyn, NY.

DESIGN: *Interplan Practice, Orlando, FL*
        David Boyce, Dir. of Architecture
        Renata Rottinger, Int. Des. Coordinator
CLIENT: *B. Philip Jones, Pres., Barnie's Coffee & Tea Co.*

In this eclectic setting, the diners can enjoy a selection of over 100 coffee drinks, fine desserts, breakfast, lunch and dinner—as well as afternoon tea! This unique coffee bar in this internationally-styled, community oriented coffee house/restaurant features more than 60 blends of coffee and teas.

Opening a cafe of this nature has been a dream of the president and founder of Barnie's, Phil Jones, since he was in charge of assorted coffee houses and bookstores more than two decades ago. This dream was reinvigorated after Jones' recent trip to Venice which explains the name and the look of La Venezia.

LA ESCARCHA

ALTO LAS CONDES, SANTIAGO, CHILE

We sometimes forget how universal a "coffee break" or "a spot of tea" can be. It seems to be so American, yet we revel in joining the natives in their coffee, cafe, caffe and kava moments in sidewalk cafes in France, Italy, Spain, Greece and even in England. These moments are especially cherished in South America and the Chilean and Argentines certainly make a religious ritual of their coffee or tea time. Wherever you go in these two countries you are sure to find coffee houses or tea salons—displays of tempting desserts and people just sitting and enjoying their "moments." La Escarcha is a 240 sq. meter shop located in the very upscaled mall in Santiago, the Alto Las Condes Mall.

According to the design firm, they realized that they would be competing with the mall design and the other tenants—"places overload with images, shapes, materials, lights and colors—each shop making a real effort to be distinguished from the rest." The designers, therefore, opted for a "pop style"—"since it is intrinsically overloaded with wood and marble and some of the walls are veneered with a Brazilian timber, Imbuya, which looks like chocolate.

Other walls were plastered and painted pink, yellow clear green or blue. The tables are made of the same chocolate colored wood and topped with black Simbawe granite. For the lighting plan, the specialists came up with an informal ambient scheme reinforced with warm fluorescents and neon accentuated borders.

DESIGN: *Acuna, Irarrazaval, Langerfeldt, Arch. Providencia, Santiago, Chile*
ARCHITECTS: *Guillermo Acuna / Renato Jiminez*
DESIGN: *Luis Fernando Moro*
GRAPHIC DESIGN: *Rodrigo Ampuero*
LIGHTING: *Monica Perez / Oriana Poncini*

HANNIBAL'S

This espresso bar/cafe is part of a chain of over 50 outlets which vary in size from 250 to 2,000 sq. ft. of space. This prototype design was completed by Core of Washington, DC and it simulates an environment "similar to a European cafe blended with a California/New York warehouse feeling." According to the designer, "The desire is to mass produce the image without giving the space a McDonald's feel."

Architecturally, the architects/designers maintained the qualities of the existing space on Connecticut Ave. and yet designed "with a feeling of textures to draw the consumer in to relax as if at home—alone or with friends." The materials that are used are simple "yet the use is complex with an exercise in transposition; metal to woods—woods to glass—glass to concrete and concrete to reality."

To enhance the warm, intimate and "arty" feeling of a Parisian cafe, there is an ever changing exhibit of artwork which showcases the work of local talent. Still, in keeping with the New York warehouse context, the window bar seating, the lounge seating and the available magazine racks all contribute to the New York "grind."

The materials used in this project include concrete and ceramic tiles, cast glass as well as wire and clear glass and cherry wood.

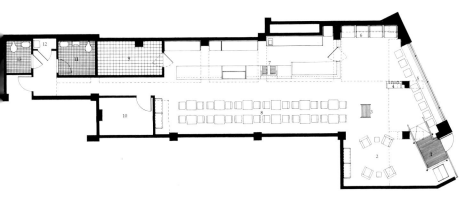

DESIGN: *Core, Washington, DC*
Robt. D. Fox, AIA / Peter Hapstack III, AIA /
Dale A. Stewart, AIA
PHOTOGRAPHER: *Michael Moran, New York, NY*

DEAN & DELUCA

WARNER BROS. THEATER, PENNSYLVANIA AVE., WASHINGTON, DC

The espresso bar/cafe located in the Warner Bros. Theater in down-town Washington, DC has been recognized for the design of this space with many awards from assorted professional organizations and publications.

The designers felt that "the space should feel as though it is an extension of the orchestra pit, but it should have the sparkle and feel of a marquee." The Dean & Deluca cafe is actually set in the space directly under the stage and orchestra pit of the theatre where it spreads out over 2,000 sq. ft. of space. The area is five ft. below street level with the food preparation located an additional four ft. below. The seating of the cafe can accommodate 56 patrons.

The architects/designers found certain structural elements in the space "significant enough to merit their use as design elements." These include the large stepped concrete piers set along the perime-ter of the space that support the stage and the orchestra pit above. "Additionally, the piers and cross beams posed the challenge of inte-grating the mechanical and electrical systems into the space." The designers solved this problem by hanging the mechanical and elec-trical hardware along and underneath the piers and beams. These exposed elements draw the visitor's eye across the cafe "creating a visual rhythm as they span the space."

In addition to ceramic tiles, stainless steel and concrete, the design-ers used bright wall finishes, reflective tiles and HID lighting fix-tures to give the space "sparkle—and add to the marquee" effect. The resulting solution is "a symbolic relationship between struc-tures, systems and finishes that creates the feel of an orchestra pit with the flash of a marquee."

DESIGN: *Core, Washington, DC*
    Robert D. Fox, AIA / Peter Hapstack III, AIA / Dale A. Stewart, AIA
DESIGNER FOR DEAN & DELUCA: *Jack Ceglic*
PHOTOGRAPHER: *Michael Moran, New York, NY*

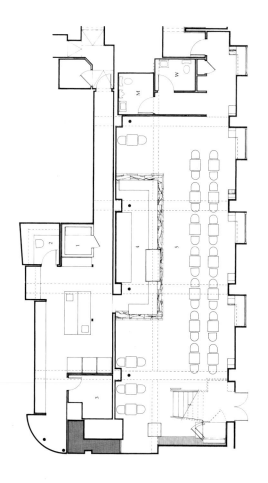

COFFEE KLATCH (RICHTUNG COFFEE)

VANCOUVER, BC, CANADA

DESIGN: *Hewitt Kwasnicky Architects, Inc.*
David M. Hewitt / Mario Simcic
PHOTOGRAPHER: *Anthony Fulker*

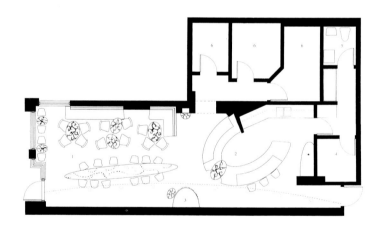

Among the famous streets of the world noted for coffee houses and shops, Robsob St. in Vancouver must certainly rank up near the top. In between the trendy and far-out shops and boutiques and the galaxy of international dining spots are coffee houses and cafes of assorted sizes, styles and looks. The Coffee Klatch or Richtung Coffee is one of them and it is located in a retail space of 1,100 sq. ft. at street level.

The client's directive was to design an upscale bar with European elegance. The architectural design firm responded by using "a contemporary vocabulary with simple, refined materials and detailing" to satisfy both the client and the context. In planning the space they did not impose a formal or structured system on the space but rather let the inherent idiosyncrasies determine much of the plan. "Together with an equally open, refined kitchen area, the coffee bar conveys an

informal unity and coherence along the lines of 'domestic' space."

Natural woods, muted yellows, terra cottas and burgundy—basically a "European traditional palette"—were used. The materials included beachwood, steel, sandblasted glass, fabric, cracked marble mosaic and an acid etched concrete floor. To reinforce the European flavor a vineyard wall relief—reminiscent of an Italian countryside in a wine grape growing area is introduced along with the cracked marble mosaic which is inset into the millwork. Though the chairs are integrated into the design in material and feeling they were not custom fabricated.

"A repeated elliptical form 'loosens' this small space functioning well in allowing comfortable movement through and around it reinforcing a continuity that creates both a feeling of accessibility and elegance."

KALDI'S

What would a trip to the old romantic and tourist ridden French Quarter of New Orleans be without a coffee shop? Usually the tourist will head for the famous, crowded Cafe Du Monde for a cup of their chickory flavored coffee and some wonderful sugar power covered beignets. But for the real or "in" crowd of New Orleans coffee drinkers the haven is just up the street on the way to the old French market (*see chapter on Markets*).

From the outside it looks like a bank that failed during the big depression and never recovered. On the inside it doesn't look that much more "successful" except to someone who wants to thoroughly enjoy a great cup of freshly brewed coffee or try some beans that are freshly roasted and ground to order. The worn, tired wooden interior is as eclectic as it gets. It looks like the tired old "grandmother" of The Mill which is also reviewed in this chapter.

Mismatched chairs are pulled up to tables of every size, style and description and then placed helter-skelter on the worn, wood planked floor. It seems as though the main source for the furniture was Salvation Army Thrift stores, garage sales and plain old discards. There is, however, a great feeling of warmth and down right comfort to be shared here. There is a low wood floored mezzanine to one side where a small jazz band will sometimes take over but mostly it is used by the habitues to while away an hour or so over the special brews and the light repasts displayed in the glass fronted, centrally-located counter. Part of the service counter also serves as seating for those who are alone or would prefer to chit-chat with strangers.

Along one wall, behind the raised mezzanine, is a fabulous display of assorted coffee beans in brass and glass containers along with shiny coffee roasters, grinders, wooden barrels, crates and cartons, and burlap bags of coffee beans.

A large central opening in the high ceiling allows the second story windows to join the tall windows that line two sides of the main level to flood Kaldi's with soft, filtered daylight. Recessed spots in the overhanging balcony and in the beams that span over the open center area add to the warm, golden feeling of the space. A giant relief sculptured figure of Kaldi dominates the stone chimney wall at the far end of the coffee house. More than anything else Kaldi's looks like a stage set for an old coffee house except that it is real and has probably served as the inspiration of many of the new "old" coffee houses appearing all over the U.S.

PHOTOS: *MMP/RVC*

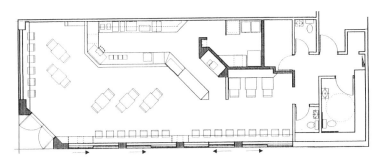

BLENZ COFFEE

VANCOUVER, BC, CANADA

This charming and intimate coffee shop is one of the growing group of Blenz Coffee shops in the Vancouver area. In addition to retailing coffee beans and "blends," the shop also serves freshly-brewed coffee drinks.

The design objective according to the president of Blenz Coffee, Geoffrey Hair, is "to create a warm, friendly service-oriented environment that will promote people to take a break from their day and relax as well as to promote the sale of coffee beans for home consumption."

To that end the 1,300 sq. ft. space is finished and furnished in solid maple woods, granite and some specialty finishes and the design of the specialty store/cafe is laid out to provide "service, space and functionality." The interior is warm and intimate, "friendly and relaxing"—all that the design firm and the client wanted it to be.

DESIGN: *Lingle Design Grp., Ltd.*
Catherine Youngern Interior Design in conjunction with
Blenz Coffee Ltd.
PHOTOGRAPHER: *Melnychuk Photography Inc., Vancouver, BC*

BLENZ COFFEE

W. BROADWAY, VANCOUVER, BC, CANADA

Like the previous Blenz Coffee shop, this new project on W. Broadway in Vancouver, is designed by Catherine Youngern Interior Design. As in the former design, the emphasis is on creating a warm and friendly neighborhood ambience—filled with "visual and tactile warmth" all to encourage "dialogue and interaction."

This shop is located in a university neighborhood which is ethnically diverse and the patrons are both single and married—artistic and many still remember the '70s cultures and find refuge and comfort in a coffee house setting. The major problem the designer, Robert Cushing, faced here was the long, narrow, "bowling alley" space. The solution had to provide visual interest and encourage traffic through the space. The designer introduced zig-zag counter seating which provides a "visual link" with the storefront windows and the long, full-length, desirable wall seating. It breaks the long run and makes "a functional interactive seating area." The lighting design supports this "pooling" to break up and create "personal spaces" along the length of the counter wall.

Throughout, the designer used a warm, monochromatic neutral scheme of honey tones, beiges and mid-browns—coffee color—with black metal accents. The millwork is natural finished maple wood and the interior wall is highly textured stucco. Since there is so much street traffic and rainy weather is not unusual, the designer specified textured and mottled porcelain tiles for the floor since it is non-skid and also easy to clean.

Two specialized retail areas are included in the space layout. The coffee bean sales area is accented with containers, espresso machines, and support product while the storefront area features small gift items such as logo-mugs, oversized latte cups and saucers, steamer jugs, table thermoses, etc.

DESIGN: *Catherine Youngern Interior Design, Inc.*
Robert Cushing, R.I.D.
PHOTOGRAPHY: *Melnychuk Photography, Vancouver, BC*

ZIO RICCO

South of the border—down Seattle way—we are in the coffee drinking capital of the U.S. where—supposedly—you can't get a bad cup of coffee since every sipper here is a "maven"—a taste expert.

When the Leonhardt Group, a graphic design firm, was called in by the client to work on what would eventually be Zio Ricco, they were astounded when informed that there would be no advertising budget. "The design would be Zio Ricco's only promotional tool" and what makes it especially difficult is that in a three block radius from its location there are at least a dozen coffee shops or houses.

Patterned after a 16th century Italian coffee house, this coffee shop features comfortable leather chairs, lush carpets, rich lighting and a welcoming warmth that encourages the coffee drinker to linger. Since graphics are so important, we are aware of the "steaming cup of coffee" and the palette of rich coffee brown tone used. The name "Zio Ricco" is Italian for "Rich Uncle" and it goes with the "sophisticated, upscaled urban gathering place, image the designers and client had visualized."

CONCEPT & ENVIRONMENTAL GRAPHICS: *The Leonhardt Group, Seattle, WA*
INTERIOR DESIGN: *Joe Stiffler*
ARCHITECTS: *Architects Reed Reinvald*

THE MILL

We may never have thought of Lincoln, NE as a "coffee house" city but on a Saturday morning—starting at 7 A.M.—there can be endless lines waiting to get into the unusual, very eclectic, The Mill for a cup of hot, brewed coffee. It doesn't hurt that the Farmer's Market only a street away draws as many as 10,000 people on a Saturday.

What started out as a small coffee shop in a back corner of a not too successful bicycle shop has now bloomed into the "in" spot in town. The warm, friendly ambience of the old bicycle shop has been "recreated" by the owners of The Mill: Duane Krepel, Dale Nordyke and Dan Sloan. The floors are yellow pine boards, the walls are covered with cedar shelves and the space is permeated with the aromas of wood, gourmet coffee and teas, and spices. The Mill is located in an old warehouse in the re-emerging Haymarket section of downtown Lincoln and the store encompasses 3,400 sq. ft. in three rooms.

The Mill's facade is mainly brick and in the style of the 1920s with windows that rise from 8-10 ft. to admit light into the woody interior. The partners added smoked glass and a brick red awning along the front of the shop. The visitor enters through a door in the center into an 1,100 sq. ft. room which is the main coffee bean sales area. Here the floors are made of oak and there are no tables and chairs to accommodate the coffee drinkers. The cedar shelves around the perimeter are covered with glass jars brimming with exotic coffees and blends. The coffee beans are freshly roasted daily in the giant, gleaming coffee roaster that shares this space. The "inventory" in burlap bags is draped and stacked on wooden pallets on the oak floor.

DESIGNED BY THE OWNERS: *Duane Krepel / Dale Nordyke / Dan Sloane*
PHOTOGRAPHER: *Ted Kirk, Lincoln, NE*

The furnishings in the coffee-drinking spaces are as eclectic and as mismatched as it goes. One of the decorative "highlights" is the Harley Davidson motorcycle hung off a column with block and tackle, metal hook and rope. It belongs to the carpenter who worked on The Mill. "A lot of the fixtures are found items that people have brought in and set up" says Dale Nordyke. It's very neighborly and kind of do-it-yourself decorating where the clientele takes an active part in the "decorating."

According to Mike Fickes in an article in Retail Store Image— "while gourmet coffee shops, large and small, national and local, often sell gourmet coffee blended with a dash of elitism, The Mill sells community, atmosphere, a place to go and meet people, a warm, comfortable social experience. It is not a coffee shop, bar or cart. It's a coffee house." A franchise deal with Franchise Consortium of Lincoln means that there may be an eclectic, warm and woody Mill heading your way!

SECOND CUP

"Coffee houses are good places to meet friends and to take a break from the hectic pace of the city," says Alton McEwen, president of Second Cup Coffee Co. "Our new design focuses on each store-community and creates inviting meeting spots, reflecting each neighborhood's unique spirit and personality through the harmonious union of art, design and music."

The building in the picturesque Mt. Pleasant area was an "eyesore"—"absolutely devoid of any architectural detail." Using the imposing exterior as a "large canvas," a team of artists was commissioned to create a garden wall. The artists' mural captures the essence of the neighborhood—"fresh and pretty"—a place where neighbors meet to chat over a fence—enjoy some coffee and conversation."

The equally dark, drab and uninteresting interior was designed to reflect the gracious homes that were built in this area during the 1920s. "A fireplace and overstuffed banquette, upholstered in a period tapestry fabric, graciously invite patrons into a space that evokes a bygone era." The service area has been positioned so that the bustle of business does not detract from the overall feeling of the shop.

DESIGN: *De Signum Planning & Design*
Karen Skobel in conjunction with
Garry Fobert: Mgr of Des./Construction, Second Cup
MURALS: *Ian Levanthat, Designs Unlimited*
PHOTOGRAPHY: *Richard Sweicz of R. Sweicz Photography*

The walls are finished with a plume and feature patterned wallpaper and the turquoise palette complements the amber wood tones used in the rounded generous moldings that were so much a part of the interior design of that era. In addition, gilded mirrors, carved accessories, a metal screen, booths and flowers all add to the homey atmosphere and a tea wagon offers fresh baked goods in a "friendly, inconspicuous manner."

Second Cup is particularly proud of this shop which is "brilliantly adorned" with handpainted floral murals by Ian Leventhal and also of the decor which "celebrates the joys of good conversation—meeting neighbors and relaxing with a beverage."

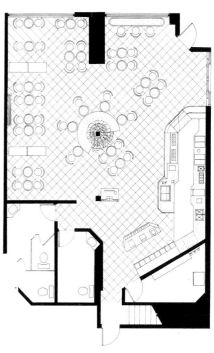

SECOND CUP

Another—completely different—Second Cup is this pleasant shop located in the ferry landing which is Lonsdale Quay. Visitors from Vancouver or residents of this revitalizing early 20th century neighborhood in West Vancouver are finding a coffee stop at Second Cup the perfect start or finish for a ferry ride.

Out in front there is a giant coffee cup/counter that projects out from the facade to serve the commuter in a rush. The shop's name is carried in a black "donut" above. For those with more time to spend and relax and that are ready to partake of some of the fresh baked products offered with the assorted coffee drinks, the circular front of the building has a pair of glazed doors that lead into the nautically-inspired interior. Here there are tables and chairs set out on the white ceramic tiled floor. The same tiles become the base for the glass faced counters that show off the baked goods. A natural brown wood faces the front of the coffee counter. On the mottled brown/copper colored walls behind the counter is a display of coffee beans and the sign boards above eye level. Towards the rear of the shop floor-to-ceiling wood shelves hold a variety of packaged foods and last minute "desserts" for the hurried commuter.

Unlike the neighborhood ambience of the Mt. Pleasant store, this one is designed to be part of the Lonsdale Quay architecture—yet it still maintains a quiet and restful separateness from the alternative coffee and dining experiences available inside the Lonsdale Market.

There are currently over 200 franchise and company owned stores.

DESIGN: *Garry Fobert, Mngr. of Des. & Construction, Second Cup*
PHOTOGRAPHER: *MMP/RVC*

THE COFFEE MERCHANTS & DR. SAM'S

The Lonsdale Market (see Markets) is located on the lower level of a two story high casual, festival-type mall which adjoins the Lonsdale Quay where ferries steam back and forth between Vancouver center and West Vancouver.

On the main level there is a coffee shop, The Coffee Merchants, which is actually an island of coffee counters and cannisters—coffee beans and pots of brewed coffees. The dark wood paneled base of the counters, the brass and glass cannisters, the green slate chalk board that serves as a menu board, and the warm incandescent lamps all add to the old fashioned image of the name. The merchandise presentation further enhances the desired feeling.

The name suggests an old musty store filled with the overwhelming aroma of coffee in burlap bags and the designers were able to capture that essence in this open space. In addition to the coffee beans the coffee devotee can satisfy his/her thirst with many kinds of coffee drinks and the "makings" are all out in view. The shop also carries a line of superior teas and chocolate drinks.

Dr. Sam's Espresso Bar is on the second level—up where the retail shops are. It brings the "coffee break" up to where the shoppers are. The above eye level, red and white vaulted canopy which is internally illuminated, is visible from almost anyplace on this level. The bright blue base firmly holds the stand in place. An auxiliary, mottled blue counter with a glass cabinet on top carries an array of "go-with" treats for the serious coffee drinker. Natural woods and incandescent lights all contribute to the sense of tradition and warmth.

PHOTOGRAPHER: *MMP/RVC*

CAFE DE LAS GALERIAS

GALERIAS PACIFICO, BUENOS AIRES, ARGENTINA

The most beautiful mall in Buenos Aires and probably in all of Argentina has to be the Galerias Pacificos which was recently renovated. This century-old building exudes grace and charm and a wealth of details of the Beaux Artes Style. The mall has a large central atrium under a fabulous dome and centered, below street level, on the lowest level is a lighted fountain—the focal point of the design. The Cafe de las Galerias is located beside the handsome curving stairway that leads shoppers from the main street level down to the lower level where the food court spreads out interspersed with more retail stores targeted at the younger generation.

"When the interior was developed for this shopping center, very much a part of the history of the city, the use of this spaceimplied a well thought out coffee shop which had to be different from the rest of the food area."

No glitz—no shimmer—no shine—no neon. The handpainted walls are finished in a gentle earthy palette to enhance the uniqueness of this sophisticated yet casual coffee shop. "The specially-designed light fittings, the arrangement of the bar and the quality of the products displayed all give definition to a store which lacks precise limits." The perimeter walls make a right angle and the light natural wood tables and bent-wood chairs with cane seats are set out on the light colored ceramic tile floor patterned in two shades of gray. A deep brown color is used on the structural column on the floor that becomes a workstation and also on the fascia above the faux painted walls.

A dark granite faces the bar and the bar is illuminated by lamps hidden beneath the black laminate counter top. The same subtle black material appears on the rear wall behind the bar. The dropped ceiling adds intimacy to the immediate area.

Wines, coffees and desserts are served either at the counter/bar where they are displayed or at the floral and peach covered tables.

DESIGN: *Juan Carlos Lopez y Asociados, B.A.*
PHOTOGRAPHER: *Favio Balestrieri*

CHARLO

SAO PAULO, BRAZIL

Charlo is a small, 65 sq. meter, fast food/take out cafe in a major mall in Sao Paulo which was designed by Arthur de Mattos Casas. The client, the owner of another very popular and successful restaurant in Sao Paulo, wanted Charlo to have the same sort of appeal: some small place would attract artistic, political and business personalities in search of a relaxed coffee break.

The original concept was to emulate the former restaurant in a smaller scale but the designer and the client both opted for this neat, sharp and efficient—"not fancy" design for the cafe. The color scheme is contrasting but still neutral; almost totally black and white from the black and white patterned ceramic tile floor to the ebonized wood, the polished "inox" iron and the counter tops of gleaming black granite. The designer has managed to keep the space open and light looking—uncluttered—crisp and sharp but still quiet and inviting.

DESIGN: *Casas, Edicoes de Design*
Arthur De Mattos Casa
PHOTOGRAPHER: *Tuca Reines*

P.A.M.'S COFFEE & TEA CO.

FAIRVIEW MALL

TORONTO, ONTARIO, CANADA

When P.A.M. decided to open up the coffee/tea/ice cream shop in the Fairview Mall, one thing was certain: they did not want to resemble in any way "the typical brown and traditional" coffee shops frequently seen in Toronto—and many other places. Even though the "Tiffany Lamp" is a signature design note for P.A.M., the feeling here had to be bright, light and contemporary. In addition the space had to be easy to maintain and still produced within a strict construction budget.

Pat Candeloro of Candeloro Designs came up with a combination of purple wood and rustic gray tones for the palette which, in turn, produced "a contemporary, tasteful and alternative appearance."

Here, a custom designed, "non-standard," Tiffany Lamp was incorporated into the design as a nostalgic note that still blends with the modern surroundings. The designer also specified copper metal and extensive tiling of surfaces so that they will not only appear fresh for years—they are also easy to clean and maintain.

DESIGN: *Candeloro Designs, Inc.*
Pat Candeloro

Candeloro and the client were both pleased with the non-traditional colors and approach to the design solution since they complement the product without appearing trite or cliche. Since the actual floor space was so limited, it was impossible to fit all the product display into the counter length of the shop. One of the storefront glazing panels opens up and allows P.A.M. to affect ice cream sales with the mall traffic.

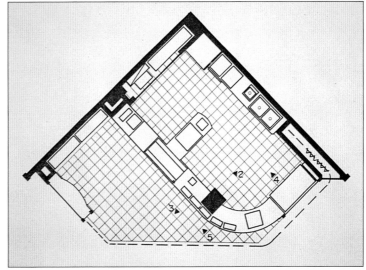

COFFEE, TEA & THEE

WHITE MARSH MALL

WHITE MARSH, MARYLAND

Though not in the Amish country, the designers of this fully-enclosed coffee/tea store in the White Marsh Mall not only adopted an Amish sounding name, they also borrowed colors, materials and graphic design elements associated with this Pennsylvania based sect. These elements create a warm, friendly and "simple" setting for the product display.

"Coffee Tea & Thee" blends, brews and vends a large variety of coffees and so the space is always filled with the wonderful aroma of coffee beans being ground or coffees being brewed for the hundreds of shoppers who take their coffee break in the wood floored and wood trimmed space. The facade is distinguished by a three dimensional kettle spout stepping out of a diamond shaped frame over a long horizontal sign panel above the entrance. The hot pink and rich cool blue accent colors are introduced here and also on the stencilled Amish design on the light wood floor which looks like an old quilt design. The fixtures are finished with a laminate of the same strong blue accented with the bright pink color.

At one end of the triangular shaped space there is an area completely devoted to coffee beans ready for grinding. They are contained in glass and stainless steel cannisters that are stacked atop a counter of the blue finish. Adjacent to this area is a small espresso bar station where shoppers can serve themselves from a selection of choice brewed coffee blends. A fluted pendant lamp of the strong pink color identifies this self-service area.

DESIGN: *Specialty Retail Concepts, Inc.,*
Winston-Salem, NC
PHOTOGRAPHER: *MMP/RVC*

At the opposite corner of the store, slatwall panels support blue shelves filled with tea in glass containers, in packages, tea cups and mugs, tea pots and other tea related items. This is the Tea Boutique in Coffee Tea & Thee.

Connecting the two ends of the store is the curved center counter with glass enclosures where assorted baked items are shown and where sales are consummated. A deep fascia follows the sweep of the bowed counter below and fluorescent fixtures are set beneath it. The shop itself and the merchandised area are illuminated by incandescent lamps set into and on tracks fixed to the ceiling.

FREDDO

Freddo is a sprawling coffee shop in the giant new mall, Unicenter in Buenos Aires. Since the "coffee break" is an important Buenos Aires tradition, and it is not limited to any specific time—other than when the coffee drinker and the brewed coffee are in close proximity—coffee shops here are usually big, uncluttered and provide an unhurried ambience for the leisurely sipper.

Freddo is mainly neutral in feeling from the terrazzo patterned floor and granite tiled side walls to the illuminated rear wall highlighted with brightly-colored transparencies of the foods and drinks available. The light looking black metal tables and chairs are accented with an ocher gold vinyl upholstery. The same gold color faces the long, sweeping bar/counter that rests on a black base directly in front of the illustrated product display.

In addition to the illuminated rear wall and the large fluorescent lighting fixture in the middle of the space there are myriad incandescent spots scattered throughout the dropped ceiling. An interesting stepped cove of translucent plastic panels—also internally lighted—steps down from the ceiling as a transition to the electrified rear wall which is so visible from the aisle of the mall.

PHOTOGRAPHER: *MMP/RVC*

CAFFE APPASSIONATO

BELLEVUE SQUARE, BELLEVUE, WASHINGTON

For the passionate coffee lover there is this charming and delightful little coffee shop/cafe located at the end of the Bellevue Square Mall on the main level. Like a small, rustic house, the copper sheeting roof extends out towards the mall line and it carries the signage. Panels of rich colored wood frame the open entrance into the cozy, warm, coffee flavored interior where the dark mahogany wood is used on the main selling counter and for the thick slabs of molding that define the architectural elements. Wall areas are painted a deep cream color—like a cafe au lait—and one of the service area walls is sheathed with mottled, terra cotta glazed tiles.

Behind the service bar there is a wall of cannisters where the coffee beans are displayed. Packaged and baked foods are presented atop the counters as well as recessed under the counter in rustic wicker baskets. Adding to the earthy textures are the many burlap coffee bags and the terrazzo floor with terra cotta colored inserts. Warm incandescent spots add to the hospitable feeling of the space which, though limited, does provide for some seating at the high round tables surrounded by black upholstered stools.

PHOTOGRAPHER: *MMP/RVC*

CAFE FONT

The coffee loving designer/graphic artist who is responsible for the total design of Cafe Font lives and works in Seattle but has founded this outpost in a mall in Anchorage where Cafe Font coffees are for sale both by the pound as well as by the cup. Odum is not only the designer—but also the owner of the coffee organization behind the cafe.

DESIGN: *Paul Odum*
PHOTOGRAPHER: *MMP/RVC*

The color scheme consists of dark wood veneers used on the curved counter that fills most of the left hand side of the almost square space. The wood also is used for the stepped shelved cabinet units which are trimmed with vermilion and ocher-camel cabinet doors situated on the right hand side of the space. The floor is brightly checkerboarded in red and pale yellow and the same red finished the plastic tops of the small tables set to either side of the space where the shopper can tarry awhile over a cup of coffee. To this palette the designer/owner has added a rich spruce green which appears over the entrance and carries the logo signage.

The "menu board" on the back wall behind the bar is patterned in the vermilion/camel and grayed deep green. The handsome logo design featuring an abstract coffee cup is also in the green color with white.

The small space is almost totally illuminated with incandescent spots either recessed into the ceiling or under the entrance sign, or on the track fixtures used to highlight the signage, the graphics and the product display.

SACRED GROUNDS

FoodLife, Watertown, Chicago, Illinois

This coffee bar kiosk is part of the fabulous FoodLife project which is reviewed in the *Food Court/Fast Food* chapter in this book.

The design concept of the total space was to make each kiosk or stand as "real" as possible. According to Martin Dorf, one of the designers of FoodLife, "It was designed as an urban park fantasy and all the food stands were conceived to showcase the preparation and display of food." Special crockery, artifacts and decor items were selected to complete the distinct personality of each stand.

The wood and marble island stands somewhat apart from the park-like setting and has a more sophisticated European quality about it. The fine mahogany wood counter that "encircles" the space is topped with a massive wood shelf that supports the black and gold sign and menu board. A round column extends from the ceiling through the shelf and becomes embedded in the counter—adding a curved line to the angular black and white figured marble counter top.

Assorted cakes and pies are displayed behind a sneeze guard while more freshly-baked products are on view in the self-illuminated, angled display case in the center of Sacred Grounds.

Small, sparkling low voltage lamps hang down from the ceiling to highlight the products while a ceiling track above with incandescent lamps makes the sign and menu board easy to see and read from any-where in the FoodLife park setting.

DESIGN: *Dorf Associates, Inc., New York, NY*
Martin Dorf

PRIMO'S

The "theater in the round" coffee kiosk featuring "Espresso Americana" created problems for the designer, Forrest Architects. "The priority for this stand-alone kiosk was to establish a presence and identity able to withstand the visual onslaught of a mall." It had to be attractive, appealing and somehow mitigate the customer's viewing of the sometimes unsightly "back of the house" functions. The kiosk also had to be capable of withstanding the wear and tear it would be subjected to in a mall set-up.

The unit was constructed of poplar wood with a painted lacquer finish for extra durability. Working within height limitations of 56 in., the designers were able to shoe-horn in all the utilitarian needs as well as the display of product requirements. A sign with a minimum profile was raised up to nine ft. without blocking neighboring tenants view lines and the designers used the trash and cream station to take advantage of another image advancing opportunity.

"The design of both the graphics and the kiosk seeks to express European substance enroute to a Hoboken roadside diner—perhaps not an inappropriate comment on America's overheated discovery of classic coffee preparation in general." The result, however, is unique and appropriate for the firm's image which did provide the point of departure for the designers.

DESIGN: *Forrest Architects, Somona, CA*

MOCHABERRY COFFEE SHOP

ROSLYN METRO MALL, ROSLYN, VIRGINIA

The Mochaberry Co. of Alexandria, VA is planning to open several new specialty shops in the Washington, DC area and they called upon Brennan Beer Gorman Monk of New York to design the prototype.

This new, upscaled and sophisticated Mochaberry image was unveiled in the Roslyn Metro Mall which, itself, has recently been renovated to attract a new, upscaled and upgraded market. The designers found their inspiration in the warm, smart and rather stylish European coffee houses/cafes and they reinterpreted that feeling in fine woods and simulated stone.

The multifaceted counter/service area/bar moves out asymmetrically from the rear service counter and both are finished in a rich dark Honduras mahogany with classic, cornice-like moldings finishing the matte black counter top. At the service end of the counter a built-in glass case shows off a variety of cakes, pies and other dessert options. The bar stands atop a satin brass base which in turn rests on the terrazzo floor speckled in assorted warm colors and black.

The rear wall—behind the bar—is finished in a chamois color and it is outlined and accented with panels and moldings of the dark mahogany wood. A deeper ocher color with black, on non-glare

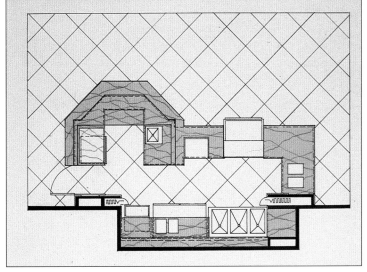

DESIGN: *Brennan Beer Gorman Monk, Interior Design, New York, NY*

acrylic, is used for identifying the menu board which is ambiently illuminated. It is located above the glass shelves of the back bar.

In addition to the light bar stools there are several round tables on the floor with open work metal chairs. They are all black as is the china—black with white trim. The lighting is provided by Halo specialty lights and the result is a successful and sophisticated coffee shop/bar with a decided European flair.

CUPPS

PROTOTYPE DESIGN

Cupps is a prototype design for a national chain of shops catering to connoisseurs of specialty gourmet coffees and teas. It was designed by Design Forum for the Woolworth's Co.

Cupps is "a bright, unique environment created to project the image and personality of the retail concept: fresh, hot and inviting." The designers have created clever contemporary signage and pictorials which they combine with sleek finishes and tile to achieve "a distinct, cohesive retail identity."

Black tables, chairs, and accents contrast with the red and white checkered pattern which appears on the white tile front of the counter and as a band on the rear wall of the open kitchen area. Coffee beans, for grinding, are for sale near the main service counter.

The designers have kept the lighting soft and restful in the actual dining or seating area of the shop while the open kitchen is highlighted with white light. "The pleasant combination of colors and finishes promises an enjoyable experience in a setting that is soothing, sophisticated and designed to rejuvenate today's time-conscious customer."

DESIGN: *Design Forum, Cleveland, OH*
Bill Chidley, V.P. of Design
Carolyn Zudell, Creative Dir. of Graphic Design
PHOTOGRAPHER: *Russell Abraham*

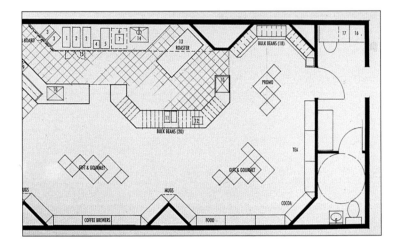

DESIGN: *SDI-HTI, New York, NY*

CAFE MIAMI

BLOOMINGDALE'S

THE FALLS S/C, MIAMI, FLORIDA

Partly as a result of the devastating effect of Hurricane Andrew on the 8-year-old Bloomingdale's store and also as a valid excuse, the retailer decided to update the design to be more in keeping with its current corporate image.

Overall the store was given a softer, lighter look that better suits the semi-tropical location. The new palette is dominated by beach and sand tones—by natural materials and warm textures.

The design elements are a blend of contemporary and update classics. The new warmer, lighter look is very obvious in the coffee shop located in the new Bloomingdale's for their customers' convenience. Cafe Miami is—if nothing else—light, bright and open. The all-white ambience—walls, floors, counters and ceiling—is accented with aqua upholstered stools and aqua ceramic tiles on the rear wall of the counter area. A very Miami pink neon light washes the fascia over the aqua wall where the Cafe Miami sign is located. More neon floods over the counter front. Black accents add to the Moderne Miami look of the cafe.

AILES COFFEE SHOP

BROSSARD, QUEBEC, CANADA

The coffee shop in this new two-level fashion specialty store is situated underneath the second level and it is framed in by the two curving stairways that are the focal elements of the floor's design. It is hard not to find this oasis which was designed by Ostroff Designs of Montreal to look like an outdoor cafe of some country inn.

Old brick, marble square floor tiles and the maple wood chairs suggest a warm, casual dining experience as do the verde gris wrought iron globe light fixtures on the bricked-over columns.

One half of the sweeping space is devoted to the cooking and serving of the food. Here the back walls are tiled in white and a brick faced oven is decorative as well as functional. The white service counter is trimmed with the maple wood and partially topped with white marble as are the black iron based tables on the floor.

DESIGN: *Leonard Ostroff Designs, Montreal, Que.*

In the seating area a mural turns the corner and it is set back behind a wood ledge and interrupted by white piers. Through the openings the diner sees trees, fountains, balustrades, period style architecture, tables, chairs and colorful sun-brellas. The diner is actually transported to some country inn—somewhere in provincial France on a sunny spring day. The track lighting over and in front of each mural panel enhances the warm, glowing, out of doors feeling.

Wrought iron gates set into the old brick piers and ivy topiaries serve as an entrance into this relaxing coffee shop in a retail setting.

JOE'S RESTAURANT & BAR

JOSEPH'S BOUTIQUE, SIMPSON'S

PICCADILLY, LONDON, ENGLAND

According to the old song—"Everybody's doing it!"—and "it" today refers to adding coffee shops, bars and food areas in the midst of the retail setting. Not in the basement—not near the roof—but right out there where the selling is done. "It" means incorporating a dining experience with a shopping experience. "It" means keeping the shopper from wandering off when she feels the need for a coffee break—or when her lunch hour is almost over and she still hasn't had a snack. "It" is a spot for coffee or tea—a snack—a light repast.

The Joseph boutiques are found in the better shopping streets in London and a new Joseph's has been added to the Simpson's specialty store in Piccadilly Circus. Part of the design of the space is the Joe's Bar which is shown here in its retail context.

DESIGN: *Joseph*

The cafe is located on a mezzanine overlooking the new, crisp and contemporary boutique which is set out on two levels of natural timber floors separated by two steps. There is a direct entrance into the street level of Joseph's where white metal fixtures and wall fittings support a display of merchandise. The shopper is invited to step up to Joe's Bar where she can sit at a white cloth covered table on a stylish black lacquered chair and look over the natural wood louvered railing down onto the selling floor—or through the oversized squares of glazing in a white metal grid onto the street below. Unusual stainless steel bar stools, topped with black leather, also provide seating at the white bar which is covered with a sheet of pale smoky toned plastic. The white walls are simply adorned with black and white photographs of Joseph and his fashions—in wide, wide mats and within walnut frames. The only touch of color is the live flower corsage on each table. The lighting throughout is sharp, clear and as bright as the space itself.

KALOGIROU

ARCHITECT/DESIGNER: *Fivos Kidoniatis, Athens, Greece*
PHOTOGRAPHER: *Takis Tegos, Photo Tegos, Athens*

PLAKA, ATHENS, GREECE

Kalogirou is a unique and historically interesting women's specialty store located in the Plaka—on the foothills of the Acropolis. This century old residence was purchased by F&C Lemonis, SA and renovated into an elegant fashion shop where the company's line of high fashion ladies footwear and related leather accessories are shown along with ready to wear and leather accessories by noted designers.

The architect/designer has retained as much as feasible of the turn-of-the-century structure and reused parts, materials and details from the original. There are pine plank floors and walnut wood exposed ceilings, as well as the gracious marble stairway with carved, cast iron railings that connects the two retail levels.

A very popular the vital part of the main level of Kalirou is the caffe shown here. The rough textured stuccoed walls are decorated with old, rose colored bricks arranged in arches and columns. One arch serves as the entrance into the caffe from the main selling area. The other walls are stained a muted terra cotta color and here too the bricks are used to outline the openings into another selling space. The brickwork faces the bar which is topped with a thick slab of wood. Behind the bar, a series of arches appears and some are backed up with blue and yellow stained glass panels.

The central hooded area holds an antique coffee burner where the traditional Greek coffee is prepared with traditional brass implements. The brewing is done in "boiling sand" to "reduce the boiling of the water and bring out the total flavor of the coffee."

Patrons can indulge in their Greek coffee habit seated either at the bar or at some of the small marble topped tables on top of antique, brass-legged bases. Shown here is some of the fine period English furniture that is used to "furnish" Kalogirou and add to the elegant residential quality of the entire retail store.

DONNA KARAN and GUESS

Here are two examples of how coffee bars are being integrated into retail design of popular shops. In the Donna Karan store—on Orchard Rd.—the white bar is located up front between the two open back display windows that face the busy traffic street. The bar shares the wall space with some TV monitors that provide entertainment for the shopper who stops for a quick coffee, juice or soda before continuing her perusal of the fashions being presented on the floor.

The Guess store is located in one of the newer malls in Singapore and here the wood finished bar is situated near the exit to the store. Someone in search of a "quick fix" who doesn't want to wander off to the food area on the lower level of the mall can step into the Guess bar without walking through the entire selling area. The natural slate tile floor, the wood strip facing on the bar and the use of natural wood and brass for accent details create a warm, casual and relaxed setting for the young-at-heart Guess shopper who wants a soft drink—a hot drink—or maybe even a quick snack.

PHOTOGRAPHER: *MMP/RVC*

REPLAY COUNTRY CAFE

In an interesting "cultural exchange" and as a classic example of how internationalized retail design has become, we present Replay Country in Soho. Stepping into this store is like stepping back in time—to the early part of the 20th century, when general stores and dry goods stores were the main retail sources and they carried bits and pieces of everything—even food. The 9,000 sq. ft. store, on two levels, explodes with a sense of Americana and a century full of popular arts. The space is crammed full of artifacts and antiques of the American retail past: the frontier, the years before and between the two World wars.

There are signs, machinery, display pieces and architectural elements and Replay Country goes almost beyond Disney in recreating the American retail past—as we would like to think it was. What makes it all so unique is that all this stars and stripes American theme was designed and installed by Italian designers and the fittings were provided by an English firm.

On the lower level—immediately upon descending from the street level—the shopper is greeted by the coffee/snack bar redolent in old fashioned metal point of purchase signs and cut outs. Like the rest of the carefully "disordered" store, there is a scattering of seating for those who would like to step up to the counter to be served. Like almost everything else in Replay Country, the old, beautifully-detailed and restored oak bar had a previous existence probably in some old saloon. Mostly coffee and espresso is served along with a selection of baked goods.

Having coffee here is like stopping at a way-side stand off some dusty old road in the midwest—50 or more years ago. It becomes part of the Replay Country shopping experience.

DESIGN: *Rodolpho Dacoma & Stefania Leonardi, Arch. Assoc., Milan*
PHOTOGRAPHER: *Eduard Hueber, New York, NY*

JERRY'S SHOES/CAPPUCCINO & JUICE BAR

DALLAS, TEXAS

The 15,000 sq. ft. "superstore" is a renovation of one of Larry's Shoes traditional locations. The objective was to create an environment that could offer the sort of sophistication one finds in most high-end, specialty stores—even though the shoes here are discounted. "In other words—create a design that communicates luxury and quality as well as discounted prices."

The store categories were departmentalized by having set themes in each area and the shoppers are invited to browse from one area to another. The real "action" is in the athletic shoe department and this is also where most of the "fun" is. Located in the midst of all that hubbub is the Cappuccino/Juice Bar where free drinks are served to visitors and shoppers alike.

The mini-bar is sheathed in bright red miniature mosaic tiles while the front of the slightly bowed bar is yellow tile with patterned inserts of the red as well as panels of blue mirror. A TV monitor supplies additional "entertainment"—even if it is all commercials and by watching the ads—the patron "pays" for the refreshment.

The bar is only one of the many amenities offered in Jerry's Shoes. The customers can have his/her shoes shined while shopping barefoot for new shoes and the ultimate in shopper-pandering is the foot masseuse who is there to rub foot aches and pains away.

DESIGN: *Retail Design Group, Columbus, OH*
ARCHITECT: *Zero 3 Architects, Dallas, TX*

LA RUCHE RESTAURANT

DE BIJENKORF, ARNHEIM, NETHERLANDS

Located in the Arnheim store—as part of the Arnheim 2000 project is the new La Roche restaurant which represents a "new approach to in-store restaurant design." It was designed to be not only a quality restaurant but a customer service as well.

According to the designers, "In devising the new concept, the challenge was to readdress the well established visual language and ambience of a fast-food, self-service restaurant—and to create a distinctive personality across a large scale, open space plan." The source of inspiration for this design came from a photograph of a 1930s Modernist cafeteria that was originally designed for the Rotterdam store by Willem Marinus Dudok. What Virgile & Stone did was reinterpret that 1930-ish imagery in the context of a contemporary setting.

DESIGN: *Virgile & Stone, London, England*
PHOTOGRAPHER: *Ian McKinnell*

The La Ruche restaurant covers 740 sq. meters (approx. 8000 sq. ft.) and can seat 210 persons around a self-service international food court. Maple wood with contrasting terrazzo and mosaics, etched glass, silver anodized metallic finishes and specially designed Lloyd Loom chairs are used to create "an understated, timeless atmosphere." One can tell from the accompanying photographs that the designers—working with the in-house design team—put great emphasis on the visual presentation of the food.

GREEN CENTER CAFE

KAISER PERMANENTE

PASADENA, CALIFORNIA

Faced with a series of unusual "goofy" spaces, the designers, Fong and Miyagawa, brought a sense of style and order to Green Center Cafe with the innovative blending of traditional and contemporary elements. The Cafe is located in the new Pasadena structure which houses the Kaiser Permamente data processing firm. "The warmth, diversity, color, comfort and the sense of 'place' is unexpected in the contract facility used for feeding health services office personnel."

DESIGN: *Fong & Miyagawa Design Assoc., Los Angeles, CA*

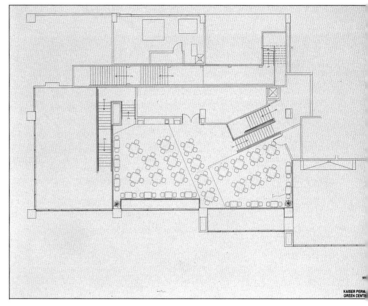

Kaiser wanted a comfortable, "boutique" environment that could be enjoyed by all but the designers were challenged by the varying ceiling heights in the space, the double loaded windows on two sides, no available outdoor entrance and a budget that definitely called for "creative design solutions." Alice Fong said, "Our goal was to mix traditional and contemporary elements in a way that made sense. We designed the space as a cafe that could evolve into a cafeteria, instead of starting with a straight ahead cafeteria design."

One of the first impressions upon entering the cafe is the casement and tie-back drapes on the 20 ft. high windows. Together with the carpet and the acoustical ceiling, they help to control noise levels. The curtains also regulate the levels of light and "definitely add residential warmth and color to the space." In addition the designers added large pendant lamps, fluorescent cove lighting and a few recessed down lights to balance the natural daylight. The resultant illumination "brings out the true richness of the colors yet remains free of 'islands' or hot spots—even in spaces where the ceilings drop to eight feet."

Since the space is open every day, maintenance and long-term durability were important considerations. Rich, inviting colored tough and serviceable vinyl fabrics were used to cover the walls and the floors are covered with a printed nylon carpet with a Pasadena Rose design which is both "sophisticated and warm." The designers included sandblast-edged glass throughout the space and even integrated motifs from the neighboring architecture into the scheme like the moldings based on the pediment and entry of an adjacent church.

Alice Fong, speaking of the Green Center Cafe, said "This is a project of the future. They challenge you to come up with innovative design solutions, to use the full resources at your disposal, and to work closely with the architects, the general contractors etc.—all to deliver a project that works for anyone."

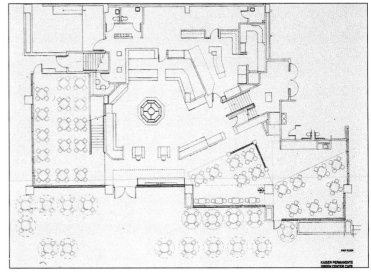

CENTER CAFE

ONE DETROIT CENTER, DETROIT, ILLINOIS

Commercial Bank is the major tenant in the noted Johnson-Burgee building in downtown Detroit and the Center Cafe is a self-service restaurant subsidized by the bank.

The designers, Meisel Ltd. Associates of Chicago took their inspiration for this cafeteria from the 1950 style delicatessens that were so popular in many neighborhoods. In an effort to recreate that warm, intimate, yet "busy-busy" feeling of these delis, the designers have created a "scramble": arcaded dividers, banded ceramic piers, wood columns, patterned linoleum floors and other "period" details.

The color palette is warm and '50-ish with a deep red/orange color appearing to dominate. The floor in front of the open cafeteria service line is checkerboarded on a diagonal in the deep vermilion complemented with a grayed green. Overhead a series of banners in oranges, reds, browns and greens span over the aisle creating an arcade. The counter itself is faced with a homey pine wood.

DESIGN: *Meisel Ltd. Associates, Chicago, IL*
PHOTOGRAPHER: *Doug Snower*

Black and white checkerboard pattern, framed in vermilion, is used to accent the signage, the menu-boards and the graphics. The walls are finished in the red, plus oranges and curry yellow as are the linoleum-topped tables. The plywood chairs, upholstered in pale green vinyl, have the bowed backs made popular in the 1950s by Eames. Booths are finished in ebonized wood and covered in red or black vinyl.

The arch or arcade motif is repeated in the L-shaped seating area where lintels with scooped-out bottoms, supported on the brightly-colored columns, span over the main aisle. The sweeping curve is also used as a "screen" between the booth seating and the aisle. Here also, linoleum-topped tables and plywood chairs are used with pendant, half-bowl, lighting fixtures and the color palette to extend the imagery of the '50s delicatessen.

GALLERY CAFE

AT&T/USG CORPORATE CENTER, CHICAGO, ILLINOIS

"The Gallery Cafe is a unique, upscale cafeteria. It is specifically designed for customer convenience and satisfaction and quick service, a large selection of fresh and home made menu items, moderate pricing and an inviting ambience are the hallmarks of this new restaurant."

Designed by Meisel Ltd. Associates of Chicago, the Gallery Cafe is situated on the mezzanine level of the AT&T/USG Corp. Center and caters to the professionals in the building and also draws on professionals in a two block radius. The Cafe can accommodate 370 patrons. Though the cafeteria is open for breakfast and lunch, it can be rented for special occasions with special, custom designed menus. The space can seat 300 for sit-down dinners and up to 700 at receptions.

The space is divided into several areas including a raised gazebo, a banquet area and an L-shaped dining room. The contemporary cafeteria style restaurant is designed to feature several different food kiosks. To provide an "elegant yet comfortable" atmosphere, the color palette is almost entirely black, gray and white. White tiles with black trim accents cover the walls and marble is used on the floors. There are black laminate table tops and gray marble tray-slides and the neutral palette is relieved and highlighted by bright multi-

colored fabrics, decorative stencil-work, light woods, natural birch venetian blinds in front of the 10 ft. tall windows and soft, relaxing lighting. An ever changing show of contemporary paintings, watercolors, graphics and photographs by Chicago artists is featured in the Gallery Cafe and customers can purchase the artwork.

The Gallery management is promoting itself as "a perfect spot for quick affordable meals in an artistic environment" and is also there to point out the location is "prime space for private parties, corporate receptions and special events."

DESIGN: *Meisel Design Group, Chicago, IL*
PHOTOGRAPHER: *Doug Snower*

SWEETPEA'S

ATLANTA, GEORGIA

Morrison's Restaurants are know throughout the southern part of the U.S. The company was inspired by the Whistle-stop Cafe seen in the movie "Fried Green Tomatoes" to open a whole new family restaurant which updates the southern roadside cafes of the 1920s which offered "down home fare" like barbecued ribs, fried chicken, mashed potatoes and banana cream pie. Morrison's invited the Cincinnati office of SDI-HTI to create the prototype design for the new Sweetpea chain.

In a 7,000 sq. ft. space, the designers created a relaxed, casual environment where 200 patrons can enjoy, at the same time, wholesome, tasty food at affordable prices. Since the restaurant is targeted at young couples on dates as well as families dining on a budget, the design offers a more polished, comfortable version of the old roadside cafe for the more contemporary clientele.

"Sweetpea's has been designed to evoke a feeling a nostalgia for a bygone era—rather than duplicate an exact style." The solid oak tables, booths and school-house chairs have a "craftsman" look.

DESIGN: *SDI-HTI, Cincinnati, OH*

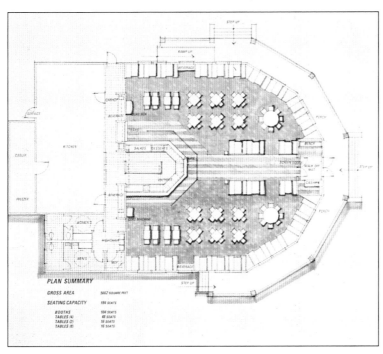

Reminiscent of the 1920s are the oak floors, floral patterned carpeting, embossed tin ceiling, neon clock and pendant lamps. Also incorporated into this heavily themed environment are period pieces like an old fashioned juke box, ceiling fans, original Coke bottles, vintage photographs and many "artifacts" of the past.

The exterior design of Sweetpea's is in keeping with the architectural designs of buildings in the South in the '20s. The wrap around porch is equipped with rocking chairs where diners-to-be can wait till their tables are available. The low, double pitched, metal roof is also a sign of those times.

The designers "aged" the facade with a thin stain that produces a "splotchy, weathered appearance." In addition—to even further the retro look—there are old fashioned commercial signs in the windows and period advertisements are painted on the side of the building and treated with a faux aging process.

In addition to the interior/exterior design program, SDI-HTI also created Sweetpea's logo, packaging, menu/match book design, employees' uniforms and other point of sale materials—"with a 1920s flavor—to reinforce the restaurants identity."

CAMERON'S

Cameron's is a new restaurant concept in Ohio and the first of the upcoming chain is located in the Northwest part of the city—an upscaled, grown sector. Each of the other operations will also feature "Contemporary American Cuisine" but each "will be different with a speciality in the food and service per location." This first project does reflect the neighborhood's look—and the upstart budget.

Basically, the space is divided in two—a bar and restaurant—and both share the feeling of a bistro. The designers were careful to provide a viewing of the total space so that though they are separate areas, they are not really apart. In addition, the dining area is further divided by a most unusual free form canvas structure which tends to set the more formal area apart from the more casual dining space which is located closer to the clatter and theater of the open kitchen. The canvas element was hand painted on site and reflects—on a giant scale—the pattern and color of the upholstery fabric used on the chairs and the booths. Throughout Cameron's the walls were painted. A hand-applied texture was added in the dining room "to provide a more intimate scale to balance the high vaulted ceiling."

The bar area is where the patron enters and through the horizontal slots in the "dividing" wall one can see into the dining room beyond. "Hard surfaces in the bar create an energy that is maintained throughout the space." Black pick-up sticks that are 3' long and monochromatic sepia prints are used to decorate the space.

DESIGN: *Design Collective Incorporated/Wandel & Schnell, Columbus O.*
PHOTOGRAPHER: *Studiohio, Columbus*

BENNY'S BAGELS

YALETOWN, VANCOUVER, BC, CANADA

Benny's Bagels is a 6,000 sq. ft. "social event" that the designer feels evokes a unique character that can be summed up with "the art of production." Not only are bagels made to eat in or take out—Benny's is also a 24-hour, non alcoholic bar/restaurant/pool hall.

Based on the theme "the art of production," a giant 60 ft. long mural in sepia tones, yellows and oranges is the focal point of the design. It depicts a factory during the Industrial Revolution. "The dynamic imagery gives you a sense of power, strength, heat and effort—all in making a bagel within the smoke filled Industrial Revolution of the time." The factory imagery also complements the Yaletown location of Benny's Bagels which is a neighborhood of wood and brick warehouses and factory buildings.

The mural's theme is given a three dimensional expression on the back bar where it becomes another important focal element. "The central boiler, made of industrial copper, is half round in shape and the red neon light that emits through the "cracks" and "seams"—"elude to the raging fire within." The design also combines function with fancy by incorporating the mechanical ducts necessary for the air supply into the "boiler"—"to form part of the charade to convince you of the reality of the situation." The round mechanical duct is faux finished in an aged copper patina to appear as part of the "functioning" boiler. Gargoyles and griffins also watch over the bar.

DESIGN: *Sunderland Innerspace Design, Vancouver, BC*
Jon P. Sunderland & Daniel Lewis
PHOTOGRAPHER: *Roger Brooks Photography, Vancouver, BC*

The designers combined steel, natural woods, faux finishes and neon accents with the warm colors and the curvilinear forms which tend to soften the space and "create a diversified environment that is comfortable and inviting, morning, noon and night."

Almost everything in Benny's Bagels was custom designed and fabricated—often in common, inexpensive materials. The bar front, as an example, is constructed of asperite chipboard and raw steel and finished with a coating of clear lacquer. Custom steel supports are detailed with exposed fasteners and take on a bowed shape.

The supports are anchored into the floor and hold the floating steel counter top and chipboard fascia panels. The pool tables were also custom designed to relate to the character of the rest of the design.

This design was recently honored with a gold medal in the Restaurant/Hospitality category by the Interior Designers Institute of British Columbia. Though there is a big stretch between bagel making and the Industrial Revolution the judges did think that the project was "great fun" and "hung together."

Casual Dining: Themes & Variations, Exhibition Kitchens

DIVE, LOS ANGELES, CALIFORNIA

DIVE

Think Steven Spielberg—think "La-La-Land" (that is Los Angeles for those who never heard the term)—and what do you come up with? It is the new, high-powered, deep "see" experience in dining out called Dive! It is where fantasy blends with fact.

It is where diners experience the sights and sounds of a spectacular underwater film adventure while enjoying the "signature tastes" of gourmet submarine sandwiches.

The concept is the brainchild of the Levy Restaurants and Steven Spielberg. The actual design is the result of creative designers, architects and consultants working together. Dive! is a two story, 11,000 sq. ft. space—the hull of a submarine with vaulted cylindrical ceilings and bowed exterior walls braced by metal ribs.

Dive!'s exterior shell is constructed of many high-tech, metals, painted in accent colors to create the feeling of an authentic submarine rising up on the street of L.A. In its search for "authenticity," a network of technical sub apparatus detail the dining area and they include pressure gauges, throttles, control panels and sonar screens.

"Porthole 'water' windows bubble and safety lights flash—activated by a sophisticated computer system as the restaurant 'plunges into the depths' once every hour during the Dive! sequence."

As previously noted, the exterior of the restaurant resembles a yellow and blue submarine with a 30 ft. yellow nose cone aimed at Santa Monica Blvd. The nose cone is complete with an "up periscope" and radar light. Fiber optic accents surround the sub and outline the four color Dive! logo on the conning tower. Set between the nose cone and the body of the sub, under an awning of vibrant blue with a wave pattern, is an outdoor dining patio.

INTERIOR DESIGN: *Meisel Associates Ltd., Chicago, IL*
ARCHITECT: *Lawrence Berkley & Assoc.*
CONSULTANTS: *Dale Mason & Phil Hettema*
PHOTOGRAPHER: *Karl Herrmann*

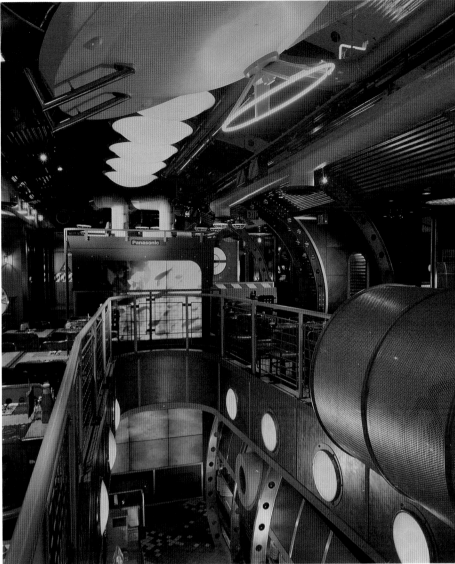

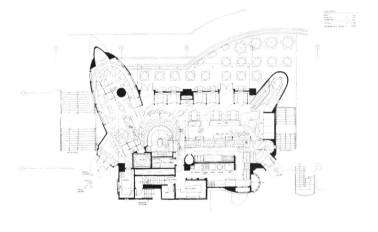

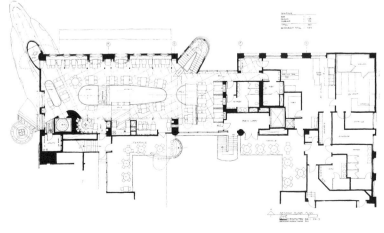

The diner enters on the first floor through an open hatch with a backlit depth gauge in the floor. A lounge area with a semi-circular bar ringed with bar stools like "torpedo tops with round targets" is tucked into the sub's nose cone and here the patron can watch the Dive! underwater adventure through porthole shaped video monitors. For those who want to get into the act, a working periscope offers a view of the neighborhood around the restaurant.

The gallery is located on this first level; an open display kitchen where diners in their "captain's booths" can watch food assembled. The booths have glass topped, torpedo tables with etched sonar screen patterns.

A 210 sq. ft. rear projection screen—visible from both dining levels—features the Dive! underwater presentation which can also be viewed from 32 other monitors located throughout the restaurant.

To get up to the "see-level" or second floor, the diner can climb the conning tower or go up in the "diving bell" elevator. In what would be the sleeping quarters of the submarine, the patrons are seated beneath exposed pipes, conduits, torpedoes and hatches of the sub's hull. "Overhead, a computerized track weaves in and out of the pipes and a fleet of four model subs circle above—including a luxury liner, research vessel, a Dive! replica sub and swimming trout."

A trip to the toilet is part of the adventure. The doors are trimmed with bright safety striping and yellow rubberized tiles cover the walls. Corrugated metal lines the ceilings.

The menu features—what else—submarine sandwiches. Here they are entrees served on crusty baguettes and includes "Sub-burgers," "Sub-stantial salads," "Vegetable Subs," and "Sub-lime desserts."

Larry Levy, chairman of Levy Restaurants says, "The atmosphere we've created at Dive! allows guests to escape to a completely unchartered environment—one that combines the tastes of wonderful submarine sandwiches with breakthrough decor and special effects which celebrate the food concept." The next Dive! is opening in Las Vegas and there should be at least ten more by 1996. A whole line of Dive! related merchandise—wearables and souvenirs—are already in the works and a retail counter should be a prominent feature in future Dives!

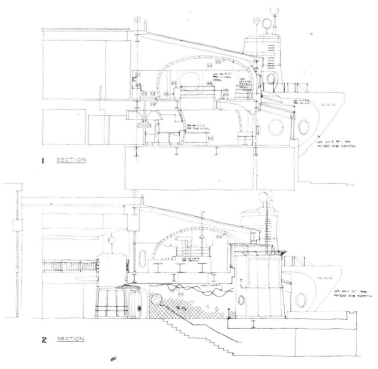

PLANET HOLLYWOOD

CHICAGO, ILLINOIS

A phenomenon of the '90s—like Hard Rock Cafe of the '80s—is Planet Hollywood: part restaurant, part cafe, part museum and part retail outlet. It is the "in" place for all ages who love the movies, nostalgia, being where "the action" is and being part of "the action."

"The central idea for Planet Hollywood designs," says David Rockwell of Rockwell Group who designs these multi-media extravaganzas," is that of creating a world in which Hollywood icons are brought to life and the patrons feel as though they're stepping right into the movies with them." This approach has resulted in a series of strongly themed casual restaurants brimming over with Hollywood memorabilia in places like New York, Aspen, Washington, DC, Las Vegas, London and Chicago—shown here.

By incorporating such one-of-a-kind collections of artifacts in every available space of the informal, relaxed restaurants, each location's collection is "a unique architectural event" to be participated in by the observer.

Depending upon the location, themed rooms are developed that speak to the particular locale. In London, the diner enters through a "gun barrel" into the James Bond room while the "Gangster Speakeasy Parlor" in Chicago has walls riddled with bullet holes. A science fiction room is carried over from location to location "as a testimony to the role of fantasy and adventure in movie lore."

DESIGN: *Rockwell Group, New York, NY*
formerly Haverson Rockwell
PHOTOGRAPHER: *Norman McGrath*

In almost all Planet Hollywoods the central focus is the main dining room and the "diorama of the Hollywood Hills with its singular combination of imagery, nostalgia, memorabilia and lighting effects."

PLANET HOLLYWOOD

WASHINGTON, DC

"Planet Hollywood has become one of the most exciting and important developments in the entertainment world and has enhanced the business and cultural life in its location cities." It is also the world's only dining experience inspired by the worlds of film and television. Every opening has all the drama, pizzazz and glamour of the old-time movie premier where a succession of film and entertainment notables show up to show off.

In addition to the extensive collection of "memorabilia (Judy Garland's Dorothy dress for "The Wizard of Oz," the mermaid's tail from "Splash," "I Dream of Jeannie's" genie bottle, Sharon Stone's notorious ice pick from "Basic Instinct," etc.) diners are entertained with preview trailers of soon-to-be-released movies. When trailers are not showing, custom designed film montages are displayed on the screens and music from movie soundtracks play in the background.

Every Planet Hollywood—and every one is different—is ablaze with color, pattern and light. In some areas, as here in Washington, DC, white tablecloths and simple black upholstery is complemented by the background of theatrical "flats" with dimensional shadow box openings for miniature sets and memorabilia.

The main room has zebra striped table covers and the sprawling mural features famous Hollywood personalities. Costumes worn by the famous are encased in display cabinets on the floor. In keeping with the Washington, DC setting there is a room devoted to the F.B.I. and crime action movies.

The menu features freshly prepared California style "new classics" like unusual pastas, exotic salads, turkey burgers, gourmet pizzas and a vast selection of desserts.

In the merchandise shop there is a variety of clothing and souvenir selections so that guests can "take a piece of Planet Hollywood home with them."

DESIGN: *Rockwell Group, New York, NY*
formerly Haverson Rockwell
PHOTOGRAPHER: *Norman McGrath*

HARLEY-DAVIDSON CAFE

AVENUE OF THE AMERICAS, NEW YORK, NY

"An American legendary style was the main driving force of the design of the Harley Davidson Cafe in New York City," says Tommy Chi, the designer of the 12,000 sq. ft. restaurant/cafe divided between two levels in a midtown New York building. "The American heritage is integrated with the lifestyle in a 'free ride' environment with a fragment of contemporary architecture."

The design team has melded nostalgia and modern elements together by the use of materials. "Natural timber contrasts with metal and the movement of lighting to give the patrons a sensation of passing through a time zone of the American legend." The cafe design is all American and patriotic. A map of the U.S. is stencil cut into the underside of the building's existing canopy and twin-V Harley Davidson signature engines introduce the light sconces that anchor the perimeter of the steel facade. According to the design firm, Harley Davidson symbolizes an era of rock and roll, movies, sports and wars fought throughout the last 90 years, and they have crammed as much of that imagery into the design with artwork, artifacts, graphics and photographs.

The bar area has an 18 ft. coffered ceiling over it. Immediately over the bar is mounted the first Harley Davidson motorcycle. Other HD motorcycles—many previously owned by celebrities—are displayed on a catwalk constructed of vertical and horizontal I-beams and metal grids. This metal catwalk delineates the bar area, the retail shop and the main dining room. Smoke machines and strobe lights, attached to the catwalk, provide "additional visual energy."

DESIGN: *Tommy Chi & Associates, New York, NY*
PHOTOGRAPHER: *Norman McGrath*

The main dining room is dominated by a prefabricated metal panel which unfurls overhead as a free floating American flag. It serves as a second ceiling and envelops diners in a "totally made-in-America feeling." Elvis Presley posters cover a whole wall in the main dining room and next to the bar to integrate "rock and roll" with the Harley Davidson history. Throughout the ground level, the lighting is "dramatic and sparkly" and focused primarily on the visual elements on the catwalk and ceiling. The ambient light is secondary, almost completely-reflected light.

The entire basement level is superimposed by images of the famous American highway, Route 66, and different cement adhesive textures combined with stainless steel indicate noteworthy American points of interest. Also, down here, there is a stage for live entertainment. A showcase in this area also displays Harley Davidson retail products which are available on the ground level. The walls and ceiling surfaces are lighted softly and evenly while the millwork cabinets are internally illuminated to create "a mushy light" instead of a dramatic one. "This emphasizes, the physical boundaries of the spaces reinforcing the more intimate atmosphere."

Throughout, decorative custom elements and light fixtures were designed and made of the motorcycle components parts to "primarily add sparkle and detail art at eye level."

STRIPED BASS

WALNUT ST., PHILADELPHIA, PENNSYLVANIA

This restaurant not only received rave reviews for the food but for the ambience as well. Philadelphians who remembered the 6,500 sq. ft. space with the almost 30 ft. high ceiling that was once tenanted by a brokerage house couldn't believe the change. Not only was Marguerite Rodgers able to tame the space, keep the original architecture and capitalize on the space's "grandness," she was also able to make it "warm, cozy and comfortable." The once intimidating dark wood, stenciled ceiling and marble columns became an essential part of the final design—"reminiscent of a grand hotel in a foreign land."

One way of making the space less "intimidating" and also make use of the ceiling height was to separate the main dining area into two platform levels. Custom designed and manufactured millwork and furniture, coordinated with towering palm trees and the marble columns also helped. The platforms establish subtle changes in height and also make it possible for diners to see out through the windows which are partially covered with swept back, unbleached muslin curtains. They add "a delicate sensual element, while intricately-patterned fabrics and carpets complement the colors—and features of the existing architecture."

DESIGN: *Marguerite Rodgers, Ltd., Philadelphia, PA*
ARCHITECT: *W. Scott Winger*
FISH SCULPTURE & SCONCES: *Bob Phillips*
PHOTOGRAPHY: *Matt Wargo*

As one Philadelphia food reviewer, Maria Gallagher, stated in the Philadelphia Daily News, "the marble pillars, the 30 ft. ceiling, colorful oriental rugs, potted palms and spectacular flower arrangements, put me in mind of a grand hotel." Chaneliers with custom pleated shades add to the soft, elegant look.

Starring in this food epic are the chefs in the open kitchen which becomes a dramatic stage setting. The exhibition kitchen is special.

It was inspired by traditional working kitchens with long center work tables. These tables are complemented by hutches, a pantry, stillrooms, and a scullery for wet food preparation. There is an in-kitchen, chef's table where guests experience the creative cooking process as "active participants in the theater-like design," a 16 ft. sculpture of a leaping striped bass, made of hand forged steel by Bob Phillips, turns a stainless kitchen hood and duct work into a piece of sculptural art.

"I try in my work to have a clear understanding of what society is wanting at the time of a project," says the designer, Marguerite Rodgers. Based on her own reactions to movies like "Casablanca" and "Indochine," she turned to Moorish wood furniture, rattan, terra cotta colored walls, earth tones for the paisley patterned fabrics and plants to create an exotic ambience. She even disguise the unattractive rest room area with sepia toned drapes hanging from a chandelier in a tent-like manner, and this also added to the overall atmosphere of the restaurant.

Neil Stein and Joe Wolf are most satisfied to be the owners of this successful, hot, hot, "sexy" "in" 140 seat dining establishment.

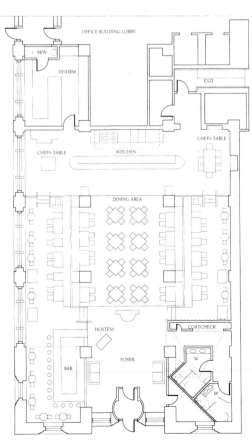

CARMINE'S CRABHOUSE

CHICAGO, ILLINOIS

Carmine's Crabhouse is a 325-seat restaurant designed by the Aria Group Architects for Alex Ana, the Chicago entrepreneur. The architecture, inside and out, carries through a Mediterranean theme and suggests an Italian coastal village. The facade is gaily decorated with bright yellow awnings, turn-of-the-century lamp post and a stone facade with arched openings "to capture the European character."

The designers were faced with the problem of a multi-leveled, 8,000 sq. ft. space. Each floor has its own variety of levels and low ceilings—"conveying a rather claustrophobic feeling." "Eliminating full height walls and visually expanding the space while creating low elements such as knee walls and lacy railings proved successful in defining areas." Eliminating levels and raising ceilings would have been too costly.

The bar area was designed with a "protruding bar seating section." A nautical look was established by the use of round "porthole" windows, draped fish netting and wood veneered surfaces. Another major focal area in the lower level dining space is the Raw Bar. The "strong visual display here adds to the dining experience" and provides a place where diners can wait for a table while enjoying their appetizers.

DESIGN: *Aria Group Architects, Oak Park, IL*
FAUX PAINTING: *Alex Darida, Chicago, IL*
PHOTOGRAPHER: *Steinkampf & Ballogg, Chicago, IL*

The Mediterranean theme is enhanced on the lower level by the color and material palette. Wood planking underfoot and oak wainscotting—reminiscent of a ship's hull—plus Italian ceramic tiles and pendant lighting fixtures are combined with walls faux finished and gently distressed in creamy beige.

A more open and airy feeling is achieved on the upper level. A custom, clam shell patterned carpet distinguishes the dining areas and the ceiling is softened with draped fabric and strategically placed arched openings lighted from above as well as skylighted areas. The new Carmine's casual setting has made it a place to see and be seen.

CHEESECAKE FACTORY

COCONUT GROVE, FLORIDA

Currently there are nine Cheesecake Factory restaurants located in the U.S. Six of them can be found in California where the company is based. The designers of previous Cheesecake Factories followed the same design concepts in creating this 6,000 sq. ft. space in Cocowalk in Coconut Grove, Florida. In each instance, each restaurant is different. Each has a different theme and is filled with original artwork and custom designed and constructed furnishings.

Throughout, the materials in this Cocowalk location are rich and natural. The flooring is limestone from France and in the bakery area absolute granite inserts are used while in the main dining room the designers specified terra cotta tiles.

Most of the walls are finished with hand painted, faux artwork which complements the solid cherry and diamond patterned cherry wood veneers that are used on the millwork. Imported black absolute granite is also used on the counter tops and bar tops and it is also used to face the cookline wall. In the bar area, 24 in. square granite tiles are laid on the floor and the table tops in the bar and dining area are made of French Cluny limestone.

Added for sparkle and a light relief are the hand carved and tempered glass panels by Trilogy of California which are used decoratively throughout the design.

DESIGN: *Hatch Design Group, Costa Mesa, CA*
CONTRACTOR: *RCC Associates, Deerfield Beach, FL*

Copper is another "natural" material that is used to add to the warmth and refinement of the palette. All light fixtures, custom fabricated, are made of antiqued copper. The ceiling fixture in the center of the ceiling cove, designed by Hatch, is made of hammered copper as are the lighting fixtures attached to the tall booths and the columns. The soffit behind the bar is copper leafed and the stemware rack is also made of copper. Copper is used as decorative inserts in the cherry woodwork. Stainless steel appears atop the booth posts and as a footrail on the granite topped bar.

Overhead, concealing the ceiling grid, are tiles covered with burgundy-colored fabric. To make this Cheesecake Factory more distinctive and unique the designers specified a mural of the "Cheesecake Goddess." Large pineapples made of fiber reinforced gypsum appear throughout the restaurant.

The designers were just as consistent in the non-food/drink service areas. Black crystalline marble is used on the floors of the bathrooms and sinks, and again the lighting fixtures are made of hammered copper.

LE FIGARO

GREENWICH, CONNECTICUT

Le Figaro—Bistro de Paris—is what this informal but authentic looking cafe means to be. Located in Greenwich, CT, it is filled with charm and charming details that have won many awards for the designer of the project, Frederick Brush.

The wide front doors that are part of the storefront design—under the red canvas awning—can be opened up, weather permitting, and the French wicker chairs and small bistro tables can be moved out to complete the Parisian side street illusion. The wrought iron balconies and the red awnings on the upper windows of the building also add to the "transplant" concept.

A sweeping, zinc topped bar, designed by Brush, is in the front cafe room. The wainscotting, where it shows, is made of patterned pressed metal sheets and the walls are either covered with two-toned raspberry striped paper or beveled glass mirrors. Etched glass partitions in mahogany colored frames serve as "room" dividers while the art nouveau linework appears throughout the space.

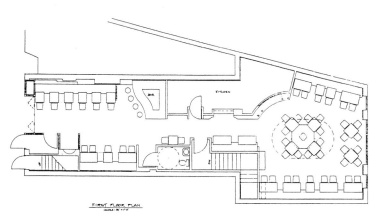

FIRST FLOOR PLAN
SCALE 1/8" = 1'-0"

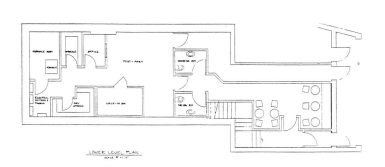

LOWER LEVEL PLAN
SCALE 1/8" = 1'-0"

Unusual is the multi-colored, ceramic tile floor inset with areas of cracked colored tile mosaics bordered in black. Throughout, the seating teams up black upholstered banquettes with curved-back mahogany stained chairs. Raised up on a four-sided upholstered banquette is Moreaux's sculpture "Reine de Pres." Behind an expanse of glazed panels and framed with an ecru balloon valance is the working kitchen which adds a dollop of excitement to the otherwise relaxed setting.

DESIGN: *Frederick Brush Design Associates*
DESIGNER: *Frederick Brush, ASID*
PROJECT MANAGER: *Jane Mielo*
TECH. RESEARCH: *Kevin Ligus*

The space is detailed throughout with typically French bistro touches such as the brass hat racks, framed covers of old Le Figaro magazines, the softly-lighted glass tulip sconces arching off the mirrored walls, and the rose bouquet chandeliers which were painted by the designer, Frederick Brush. Le Figaro can accommodate 69 persons on the inside in the two dining areas and an additional 24 on the sidewalk cafe—weather permitting.

BISTRO ZENITH

BOCA RATON, FLORIDA

The 4,900 sq. ft. Bistro Zenith was designed by Zakaspace Interior Space Planners for "Crazy from the Heat Inc.," a.k.a. Craig and Karin Larson. It is located in the Regency Court in Boca Raton, FL and arranged in an open cafe style plan.

Black gloss wall tiles surround the open kitchen and bar area and laid on the floor of the bar and dining areas are 17 in. square bone ceramic tiles outlined with 2.5 in. square black ceramic tiles. In the private dining room the designers specified a checkerboard pattern floor made of 18 in. squares of black and ocher colored carpet. Throughout, a faux paint finish was applied to the walls.

Lighting plays an important part in the design of Bistro Zenith. Wall sconces in aluminum/brass have the name "Zenith" laser cut into the faces and in the dining area acorn globes under the ceiling fan provide most of the illumination. In the private dining room the light cove around the ceiling fans is provided with incandescent and fluorescent lamps with acetate gel filters. For featured and accent lighting in the restaurant there is the large neon sign that identifies the kitchen. Nine gold-tone aluminum pendant heat lamps hang over the food counter. In addition, seven pendant halogen lamps with black shades are suspended over the bar and pastry case. The mirror behind the bar is bronze tinted.

DESIGN: *Zakaspace Int. Space Planners, Ft. Lauderdale, FL*
CONTRACTOR: *RCC, Deerfield Beach, FL*
PHOTOGRAPHER: *Steinkamp/Ballogg, Chicago, IL*

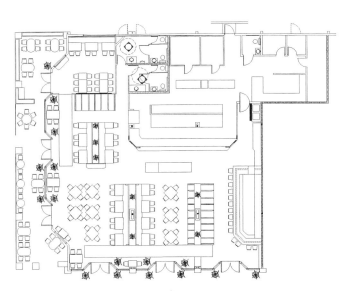

The seating in the dining area combines banquettes and pullman style booths with the tables. The booths have maple wood on the exposed posts while the upholstery used is either a waterfall or pinstripe fabric. To match the dramatic black gloss wall tiles the banquette booth seats are upholstered in black vinyl. The dining room chairs are covered in moss green and coral which are the main accents in the otherwise neutral color scheme.

MARCHE

W. Randolph St., Chicago, Illinois

DESIGN: *Jerry Kleiner, Kleiner Design, Chicago, IL*
PHOTOGRAPHER: *Mark Ballogg*

Jerry Kleiner, the co-owner of Marché, masterminded this "total concept restaurant"—from floor to ceiling—from the entrance through the kitchen. "Kleiner's designs are big and bold in this luxurious homage to the European brasserie."

Marché specializes in French bistro cuisine and Kleiner created the European brasserie ambience in the 10,000 sq. ft. space located in the hustle and bustle of the Randolph St. Market district which is one of the oldest wholesale produce markets in the Midwest. The comprehensive design aesthetic emphasizes drama and invention and at the same time is comfortable and functional. His concept for Marché "strongly acknowledges classicism while making leaps into contemporary surrealism."

Patrons enter through 10 ft., hand carved mahogany entrance doors and are greeted by the state-of-the-art kitchen which provides the restaurant's drama, theater and entertainment. The other attraction up front is the undulating 78 ft. granite bar. Hand-forged steel table bases are teamed with linen upholstered, skirted steel chairs and jewel-tone upholstered banquettes. Over a dozen Chicago artists were commissioned and then given carte blanche to decorate the massive floor-to-ceiling columns spotted throughout the space. They were encouraged to create their interpretations of European culture.

According to Kleiner, "Marché combines art, design, structure and function." It is "a restaurant that merges drama, comfort and fantasy to create a perfect setting for chef Michael Kornick's cuisine."

"The involvement of the kitchen with the guest is part of the scene" and thus he has made an attraction of what is going on in the kitchen by "creating a circus around the food." In addition to the charcoaland wood burning rotisseries, there is a Fruit De Mer bar left of the entrance (dividing the cafe from the main dining room) and also an expansive display of marinated vegetables next to the shellfish bar.

SUSHI KINTA

HYATT REGENCY HOTEL

SAN FRANCISCO, CALIFORNIA

The 800 sq. ft. space located in the Hyatt Regency Hotel in San Francisco is very small, very angular and quite long. With all of these problems to overcome Ohashi Design was able to renovate the existing restaurant into this warm and inviting space.

"Everything was done to make the interior space a focal point for customers against the glass exterior wall of the space." To create a "mood of casual elegance" the designers used light-colored wood cabinets against strongly-colored walls. The simple counters are white maple with plastic laminates and they are complemented by the almost midnight blue walls. To further enhance the feeling of intimacy and comfort, cable suspended, low voltage pendant lights were lowered from the deep blue ceiling and bronze mirrors were added for sparkle, reflection of light and decorative interest. The existing tile floor and glass walls were retained in the design make-over.

Sushi Kinta has taken on a whole new look and has also attracted a whole new clientele of sushi devotees.

DESIGN: *Ohashi Design, Architects, Oakland, CA*
Alan & Joy Ohashi
PHOTOGRAPHER: *John Sutton*

CHRISTER'S RESTAURANT

W. 55TH ST., NEW YORK, NY

Christer Larrson, the chef/owner of this 3,500 sq. ft. restaurant wanted a setting that would provide the right casual and informal ambience for the Scandinavian/American menu he had to offer. The design, prepared by Haverson Rockwell, provides "comfortable, unpretentious surroundings" that are touched with a soupcon of smart sophistication. Like Larrson's cooking style which is "back to basics," the new restaurant resembles a sort of extended mountain lodge near a body of water. Rather than being purely Scandinavian in focus, the Pacific Northwest was used to "interpret his vision." Each room of the "lodge" has its own identity and look.

The 130 seat restaurant is filled with rustic textures—done with style—from the compact vestibule, into the spacious front dining room which is cozily crowded with wood tables and chairs, a single "grand banquette," the expansive smorgasbord display and the bar. The white plastered walls are finished with log ends set into them and the bar stools are "twiggy"—adding to the provincial flavor of the room. Connecting the front room with the two rear ones is a 40 ft. long "covered bridge" tunnel sheathed in rough planking.

The entrance is marked off by a pair of blown glass fish sconces which are mounted on brushed stainless steel panels. To amuse the diner in passage there are country artifacts and old fashioned photos of fishermen. The floor of the "bridge" is painted bar red.

Fish and fishing are also recalled in the front room where, suspended from the ceiling, are dozens of hammered copper ovals which look like fish scales—or like "a school of fish swimming in sunlight."

The focal point of the main dining room is the massive stone fireplace with its wood slab mantel. Here, peeled logs form a dropped ceiling and the banquettes are upholstered in a blue plaid fabric which suggests the wool shirts worn by outdoorsmen. This area is highlighted with bright colored accents: the chairs are stained yellow, orange, green and blue—the colors that appear in the blue plaid fabric.

DESIGN: *Haverson Rockwell, Architects, New York, NY*
David Rockwell & Jay Haverson
PHOTOGRAPHER: *Paul Warchol*

The last dining room is referred to as "The Porch" and here the designers infused the space with a bright, airy quality "reminiscent of the seashore." The illumination from above and from the skylights in the ceiling is diffused by "billowing swags of sail cloth." The blue painted floor is stenciled with fish—like the sea, and the walls are paneled with painted P wood to suggest old pine planks. Adding to the outdoors feeling are baskets, bird houses, and more old photographs of fishermen and their catches.

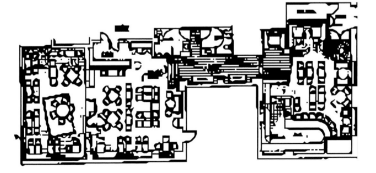

HI-LIFE RESTAURANT/LOUNGE

FIRST AVE., NEW YORK, NY

What the Rockwell Group had in mind for the design of Hi-Life was to recapture the essence and innocence of the 1940s. They made their initial statement of intent on the black and steel facade of the building which is located on the upper East Side (E. 72nd St. and First Ave.) with large, neon-lit, stainless steel letters punctuated with neon martini glasses—"echoing the hot spot's name in a naughty-but-nice '40s way."

The 2,000 sq. ft. interior is not slick and as hard-edged as the exterior. In contrast it is warm, clubby and intimate with dark green leather walls tufted with brass nailheads in the shapes of clubs, spades, diamonds and hearts. The leather areas are separated by dark, mahogany panelled areas. A vintage mahogany bar is set in a raised area behind a line of cozy, semi-circular, Hollywood-style booths—the ones we remember from the old black and white movies.

Oversized art deco mirrors are interspersed throughout the restaurant/lounge and the designers added old fashioned light fixtures from an even older cruise ship to light the way past the booths on either side to where the marlin trophy is mounted on an end wall. "The marlin simultaneously anchors the space and points towards the dining area on the left."

The cozy, club-like atmosphere of the bar continues into the dining room. Reiterating the exterior signage, the dining room's interior entryway is designated by "Lounge" written in bold, gold-leafed letters. A whimsical note is a mural screen of four seated, card-playing dogs. Replaying the muted colors of the mural's palette, rose, mustard and brown are used in a patchwork patterned fabric to upholster the seats. Dark green leather is used for the booths.

DESIGN: *Rockwell Group, New York, NY*
David Rockwell

CAFE CENTRO

MET-LIFE BUILDING

PARK AVE., NEW YORK, NY

The basic concept behind Cafe Centro was to "recreate the feeling of a Grand Cafe reminiscent of New York and Paris during the 1930s—a restaurant that could be a place for the masses—bustling with life—a place that could be ageless."

At the entrance to the restaurant—to the right of the bar area—is a mural painted by the project designer as a "dedication" to Lempika's artwork of the 1930s. The mural encompasses many of the artist's original characters but her Adam and Ever are, here, dressed in contemporary clothes and a flower has been replaced by a martini glass. The setting for the mural is a glamorous cocktail party—"evolving from New York to Paris."

The terrazzo floors in the almost 11,000 sq. ft. restaurant are inlaid with art deco patterns in alabaster, ebony and rust and the silver colored marble, where it is used, is trimmed with the rust.

The columns are highlighted with bas reliefs of fish, fowl and other creatures of land and sea—all finished with gold leaf. Custom designed, Lalique-like chandeliers of assorted designs are used to illuminate the dining space and the ceiling is fitted with large expanses of glowing anegre wood inserts.

As with many of the other elements in the total design scheme, the chairs are original and they are covered with a rich, chocolate brown on the face and with an art deco fabric in shades of raspberry, teal, persimmon and taupe on the back.

An important part of Cafe Centro's design is the display kitchen which protrudes into the dining room and it is flanked on both sides by cooking stations. Brush designed it as part of "restaurant as theater": the kitchen appears like a glassed-in, thrust stage with a scrim wall of window broken by a huge entrance for the wait-staff. To the right of the kitchen is a cast fireplace with a giant Tuscan rotisserie. To the left is a spectacular display of desserts.

DESIGN: *Frederick Brush Design Associates*
ARCHITECT: *Roberto Magris & Frederick Brush*
MURALS: *Frederick Brush*
PHOTOGRAPHER: *Roy Wright*

ROYAL THEATRE, MEZZANINE

LONDON, ENGLAND

Virgile & Stone of London was delighted when the Royal National Theatre commissioned them to redesign the main restaurant located in the mezzanine space of the theatre. "As well as providing an exciting new service for theatre-goers, there was the great opportunity to create a destination restaurant—to attract brasserie customers during the day from major corporations and to compete with top London restaurants at night."

Mezzanine is an informal, cosmopolitan brasserie which consists of a casual bar and snacking area and also a more formal waiter service, seated restaurant. A "theatrical reference" was needed to tie the dining room with the location so Jon Turner of Virgile & Stone's office conceived the 43 ft. long mural which stretches over the deep, muted green banquettes along the rear wall. The double tiered design illustrates dozens of stylized Greek gods and goddesses dressed as dancers, actors, singers and musicians—in an historic panorama of periods. The artwork was done as a series of painted panels executed by the scenic artists of the Royal National Theatre, and then set in place. A perpendicular wall adjacent to the mural is mirrored to further enhance and enlarge the impact of the unending procession of entertainers in a cavalcade of entertainment.

The designers also specified beech paneling with a distinct horizontal grain for use on some of the other walls in this 2,000 sq. ft. space. A line of exposed concrete, near the ceiling, creates an unusual molding effect. Panga Panga wood is used for the flooring as well as for the wood table tops—"to the advantage of the room's clean-lined simplicity." The ambient and task lighting in Mezzanine is provided by the table lamps, the low voltage down lights and the wall-washing fixtures.

DESIGN: *Virgile & Stone, London*
Carlos Virgile / Nigel Stone / Frances Williams / Rachel Toomb
PHOTOGRAPHER: *Ian McKinell*

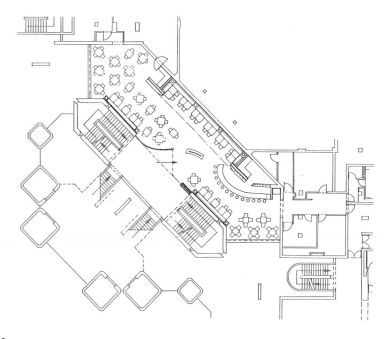

A sweeping, bow fronted expanse of glass puts much of the restaurant on view. Accent colors were lifted from the mural to spice up the interior and the mural design was adapted for Mezzanine's logo and graphics program.

GRAMERCY TAVERN

NEW YORK, NY

The architects, Bentel & Bentel, attempted "to reconcile the monumental scale of the existing Beaux Artes building (a century-old, former department store located off Gramercy Park) with the smaller domestic scale that constitutes a fundamental aspect of early American tavern architecture." In creating Gramercy Tavern the architects/designers managed to "establish a series of architectural episodes that rely on the rustic qualities of early building traditions" that fit within the uniformity of the 20 ft. square bays of space in the regular structural steel grid of the 10,000 sq. ft. of space. "By combining these two we sought to create a hybrid interior that is at once reminiscent of the past while being firmly rooted in the present."

A "horizontal datum" (unifying belt) was established that binds the various public parts of the tavern compositionally. The designers set the "datum" low—to recall the typical ceiling height of early domestic buildings. "This allows patrons the pleasure of long vistas through the various rooms as well as ease of movement." Above the "datum," the ceiling heights, shapes and materials change from room to room—depending upon the desired character of the area.

Up front is the beamed tavern/bar room which is clearly seen from the street. Above the "datum" is brilliant mural and below the area is dominated by the gently-curved, brushed copper and black stained oak bar. The mural, over 70 ft. long, by Robert Kushner colorfully depicts abstract fruits and vegetables. Making the transition from this area to the three more formal dining rooms beyond, is a large brick rotisserie and exhibition kitchen area which can be observed from most places in the restaurant. A wide, low-ceilinged corridor extends from the narrow entrance—through the tavern/bar—past the rotisserie and kitchen—across a threshold framed by two black stained oak wine cabinets—and into the dining areas.

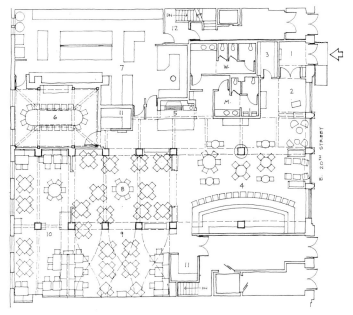

DESIGN: *Bentel & Bentel, Architects & Planners, Locust Valley, NY*
Peter Bentel / Paul Bentel / Susan Nagle / Carol Rusche
PHOTOGRAPHER: *Eduard Hueber, New York, NY*

Although the ceiling shape in each room is different, all are interrelated to reinforce the formally-shared function of the three spaces. The arches along the side walls of the first room extend across the second dining room ceiling to form cross vaults. The private dining room, of all three, most conveys the feeling of a small scaled domestic room and though it shares the color and material palette with the others, it is visually separate and apart. Wood, leather, copper and vases filled with fresh flowers are used throughout.

The custom designed furniture "underscores the distinct character of each room while at the same time linking one room to another." The banquettes in the second and third rooms reinforce the "intimate yet formal character" and they are larger versions of the loose seating up front which contributes to the "informality" of the tavern/bar space.

The visual presentation of food is a visual highlight in Gramercy Tavern. Many of the foods are cooked in the open rotisserie and they are first presented to the guest before being returned to the display table to be carved. An extraordinary selection of farmstead cheeses are shown on an antique American farm table along with a variety of breads and fresh flowers. The cheeses vary with the season and a printed menu guides the diner through the selection process.

The client, the noted restaurateur Danny Myer, and the designers Bentel & Bentel have created a dining experience that will transport their guest "to a gracious setting that blends the genteel warmth of the countryside with suave urban energy and mixes authentic, early American folk art and furniture with modern craftsmanship, furniture and art." Gramercy Tavern aims to become "a timeless New York institution."

THE KEG

LYNWOOD, WASHINGTON

The Keg is an established restaurant with outlets located throughout Canada, Washington and Oregon. In their expansion in the Pacific Northwest the company acquired this site in Lynwood for which the Mithun Partners have created this new look.

Since the site is located off a major arterial road leading from the I-5 freeway to an expansive regional retail center, the design firm opted for the concept of "building as billboard." This addresses the visibility/identity and access issues posed by typical arterial locations. The designers/architects developed a "kit of parts" design concept for this new prototype so that it can be repeated and adapted to future sites. "Familiar and flexible forms can be massed differently for future sites and different skins can be applied to regionalize each facility."

The 7,125 sq. ft. interior is designed to seat 180 patrons in the dining room and there are an additional 80 seats in the lounge.

The interior contrasts with the "rough shell" exterior and the casual lounge area emphasizes a local theme in the decor to enhance the relaxed, social, neighborhood environment of The Keg.

DESIGN: *Mithun Partners, Seattle, WA*
Doug Leigh, AIA / Stephen Cox, AIA
INTERIOR GRAPHICS: *Kim Munizza*
PHOTOGRAPHER: *Colin Jewell Photography Studio, Vancouver, BC Canada*

The major visual focus of the dining room is the exhibition kitchen which provides an on-going, coming and going entertainment. It is complemented by the color, action and presentation at the signature salad tender and salad bar. Another visual highlight in The Keg is the fireplace which the project architect describes as looking "like a 5-year-old kid did the bricklaying."

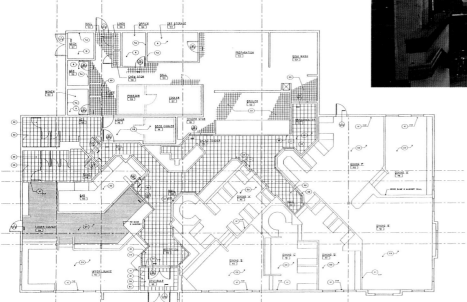

BERTUCCI'S BRICK OVEN PIZZERIA

AMHERST, MASSACHUSETTS

The 7,000 sq. ft. undifferentiated space was formerly a showroom and maintenance garage for an auto dealer but it did offer a column free and high bay warehouse kind of space with exposed steel trusses. The designers Elkus Manfredi's approach emphasized the existing room structure wherever possible. "Through the creation of theatrical 'sets,' the design created an intimate scale appropriate for a dining environment and suggests in abstract form images of Tuscan architecture and furnishings." This imagery was enhanced by abstract and pictorial murals and with faux finishes representative of the Tuscan colors and materials.

Colorful glazed tiles were used in the food preparation areas which are open to public view as they serve as backgrounds for the Tuscan "sets" in the dining area. A Mediterranean storefront is represented in a hand-made, glazed tile wall "mural" and it becomes a warm entry into the smaller function dining room.

"The juxta-position of the theatrical sets against the warehouse character of the steel trusses, exposed mechanical systems and theatrical lighting—in addition to the highly visible pizza ovens and pasta kitchen—results in a lively and informal environment which satisfies the client's fundamental requirement—that dining in this restaurant be fun."

DESIGN: *Elkus Manfredi Architects, Ltd., Boston, MA*
    Partners: David P. Manfredi, AIA / Howard F. Elkus, AIA
PROJECT MANAGER: *Robert M. Koup*
PROJECT ARCHITECT: *Amy L.F. Whitmore*
CUSTOM MURALS: *Julia Clay*
PHOTOGRAPHER: *Richard Mandelkorn*

BERTUCCI'S BRICK OVEN PIZZERIA

WALTHAM, MASSACHUSSETS

Though the first Bertucci opened only ten or so years ago, the idea of an authentic Italian restaurant in which patrons can experience the process of pizza-making in the traditional method in wood burning pizza ovens has rapidly spread through New England and along the East Coast. The Waltham location, shown here, was the first of many designed for Joseph Crugnale by Elkus Manfredi Architects of Boston.

The first goal was stated above and it was followed by the desire to enliven the dining experience and improve on acoustical privacy without sacrificing the visual connection to the food preparation area. One solution for the sound problem was to divide the space into smaller "more intimate rooms." "A vocabulary of wood trellises, screens, shutters and wrought iron railings was established to provide the required physical enclosure without sacrificing the views."

Special attention has been given to lighting. A warm, general ambient illumination is provided but special feature areas are highlighted. "Adjustable recessed incandescent fixtures accentuate the color and texture of the brick on the pizza ovens; low voltage halogen fixtures bring out the sparkle of glassware and bottles; wall washing light coves and troughs emphasize custom glazed finishes; and other decorative lights are used to recall lighting typical of courtyards and twinkling stars." A state-of-the-art dimming system permits these unusual theatrical effects.

The 6,500 sq. ft. space can seat 152 patrons in three separate dining areas which are organized around a slate tiled "street" that runs through the pizza preparation area. Diners are invited to walk along the "street" and watch the constant activity around the two brick ovens. The fully-furnished restaurant opened 20 weeks after the start of the design.

DESIGN: *Elkus Manfredi Architects, Ltd., Boston, MA*
PHOTOGRAPHER: *Richard Mandelkorn*

BERTUCCI'S BRICK OVEN PIZZA

ORLANDO, FLORIDA

DESIGN: *Elkus Manfredi Architects, Ltd., Boston, MA*

Another opening—another show! Another clever adaptation of a design concept adapted to the particular structure and location. Here, in the land of Disney—a fun, fantasy tour of old Tuscany along with the sights and smells.

As shown in the previous two Bertucci projects, "each design utilizes the existing building's volume and structure to its fullest, creating dramatically different and memorable spaces, but remain true to the brand identity." In the Orlando Bertucci restaurant we see still another juxtapositioning of signature design elements, created by Elkus Manfredi; mosaic tiled floors, slate, rusticated Roman brick, granite, woodwork stained with custom mixed aniline dyes, pigmented plaster columns with faux finishes—"all Mediterranean in flavor." In each location the decorative and given structural elements are used in various combinations to produce a distinctive look for each site.

The main, central space of the Orlando restaurant simulates an open courtyard or piazza surrounded by assorted buildings. Shutters, painted signs, protruding awnings and timber as well as overhanging fluted lamp shades all add to the Mediterranean village imagery.

The rear wall, pave in brick, houses the active pizza ovens and they, along with the open kitchen provide the entertainment and the fabulous aromas that emanate from there. A single story structure with a raised balcony contains the small bar to one side of the courtyard. A glazed tile entrance way leads to the service area.

Growing up amidst the green covered tables and the black and orange wood chairs set out on the mosaic and tile patterned floor are palm trees that seem to reach up to the sky—which is the ceiling painted a rich, deep blue color. Swooping between the trees and the painted "houses" and over the sitting area are long electric cords dan-

gling small glass lamp shades that add sparkling highlights to the piazza setting.

The same feeling is introduced on the outside where sharp turquoise awnings and dark green shutters punctuate the pale, pastel pink textured facade that is accented with a bright red/orange color.

An open-to-the-street service window for take-out pizzas is given prominence by the colorful graphics in the arch shaped opening over the corrugated awning that shields the red/orange take-out counter on the corner. White chairs, tables and sun-brellas turn the sidewalk out front into another outdoor cafe.

PAPA-RAZZI'S CUCINA

NORTHSHORE MALL, PEABODY, MASSACHUSSETS

Though this restaurant was the first of a generation of the Back Bay Restaurant Group, it is quite unique in its open relationship to two major retail stores: The Express and The Limited. Elkus Manfredi designed the base building as part of an anchor pad for these stores and was then commissioned to design Papa-Razzi's Cucina which interacts with them.

What resulted is a "casual and urban dining experience with multiple levels." The space is dominated by the undulating columns that rise up to and pass on through the mezzanine seating area. The same snaking lines appear as vertical dividing fins on the window wall with slatted trellises with waving tops and bottoms that create a horizontal movement in the design. Myriad low voltage lamps are suspended down at varying levels from the high ceiling where bands of black stretch across the long, narrow space.

The designers used a hot palette of peach, melon, and tomato red which was combined with cherry-stained woods and accented with semi-gloss black. The same steamy, analogous colors, complemented by green is used on the fabric used to upholster the banquettes and booths. The floor is divided into boxes diagonally set from the axis of the space, and here too the same colors are used.

A stairway leads to the mezzanine seating while at the opposite end of the space there is a raised area where the counter and some additional tables are set apart. In addition to the colorful signage, there are brilliant graphics that add to the energy level of the fun space that appeals to the younger shopper/diner.

DESIGN: *Elkus Manfredi, Architects Ltd., Boston, MA*

LUCCA'S PASTA BAR

BELLEVUE SQUARE MALL, BELLEVUE, WASHINGTON

In a narrow and quite small mall space of 1,300 sq. ft. the architect/designer, Kate Dutcher, came up with this solution for Lucca's new concept in mall dining: "a fanciful interpretation of historic Italian design components, interesting materials, a menu with high quality ingredients—all served in a non-sterile environment."

It starts with the action up front. The food preparation area is at the storefront—behind glass dividers—and "the food preparation becomes a stage for observing and ordering." Not only the action, but the aroma that escapes through the opening into the mall makes this a strong selling point of the design. As for the design, it is eclectic. The architect combined materials that recall Roman architecture: granite, stainless steel, ceramic tile and imported Italian lighting fixtures. Together they contribute to making this a unique and somewhat sophisticated fast food restaurant. The plan is open, and the cooking is done both in full view of the diners either up front or in the rear of the servery. The service bar/counter angles in as it moves from the entrance to the rear of the space—allowing for some small tables to share the limited space.

DESIGN: *Kate Dutcher, Architect, Seattle, WA*
Kate Dutcher and Scot Fedje

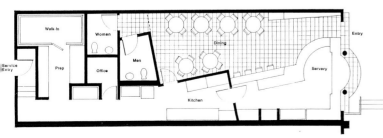

COCO-PAZZO

HUBBARD ST., CHICAGO, ILLINOIS

Pino Luongo is a well known restaurateur and has over the years worked with the architects/designers, Rosenblum Harb, in creating exciting restaurants. In preparation for opening a 4,600 sq. ft. restaurant with a pizza oven and bar, on Hubbard St., he again called upon the New York design team who created the successful Coco Pazzo in New York. They were to come up with a new "theatrical" dining setting in this former warehouse space.

James Harb adapted the aesthetics of the existing industrial space to create the sense of Dining as Theater. Textures and theatrical effects are combined to fill the space with eye-filling visual experiences and the diner becomes a participant in the theater as he/she watches the food from preparation to presentation.

As an overture, the patron enters through a vestibule designed as an Italianate garden pavilion constructed of rough hewn posts with a vaulted ceiling. In the dining area the rough timbers are highlighted to create a series of dining bays "through which diners can see and be seen." "Rich draperies and spotlights mounted on tie rods further define the stage-like qualities of the bays."

DESIGN: *Rosenblum/Harb, Architects, New York, NY*
LIGHTING DESIGN: *Johnson Schwinghammer*
PHOTOGRAPHER: *Karant & Assoc.*

To create more intimate dining alcoves, the cobalt blue velvet drapes can be closed.

The "proscenium arch" in this theater of dining frames the grilles and pizza oven with its varied blue ceramic tile veneer. It is located behind the bar and becomes the stage where the show goes on with few pauses or changes of scenery. The handsome bar is an "antique" with an old Chicago provenance and it was refinished to work in the design scheme.

The floors are laid with Australian cypress wood with inset strips of terra cotta tiles along the beam lines. The walls, to add to the texture of the old warehouse setting, is finished with Venetian plaster and complemented with sandblasted brick.

SPAIN

CRANSTON, RHODE ISLAND

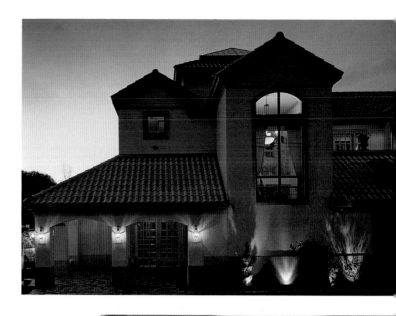

The design firm, Judd Brown Designs, worked closely with the young Spanish-born client to achieve a "mutual objective of authenticity of design and character, while simultaneously working towards a fresh '90s twist which would reflect the energetic spirit of the owner." The result, shown here, is Spain and it is the third of a series of restaurants with that name.

Conceptually, the design intent of this "ground up" project was to reinterpret the Spanish style hacienda. With its terra cotta roof tiles and the cool, unadorned stucco cladding, the restaurant is "an inviting oasis which challenges the hectic commercialism of its setting." Vital to the design is the centrally located, two story high, atrium/courtyard. The central axis of the courtyard dining room culminates in an expansive, richly-tiled wall fountain. "The refreshing sounds of running water and the colorful display of tile pattern can be experienced from each of the more intimate surrounding dining salons."

Each space carries its own personality and provides an "unpredictable and multi-experimental atmosphere—a cohesive balance of elements that serve to maintain the whole." The designers selected what they called a palette of "edible colors" to unify the spaces: cream, cantaloupe and honeydew green. To this was added intricate custom metal work, woodwork and the lighting.

DESIGN: *Judd Brown Designs, Warwick, RI*
MURALS: *Anthony Sanini*
PHOTOGRAPHER: *Warren Jagger, Providence, RI*

SECOND FLOOR PLAN

FIRST FLOOR PLAN

Rattan furniture is mixed with upholstered cherry wood elements while overscaled murals and artwork "serve as windows to the Spanish culture." They help to reinforce Spain's sense of place as do the architectural elements such as open balconies, outdoor terraces and the arched arcades that invite the natural light to penetrate and also link up the interior space.

What Judd Brown did was provide a total stage setting for the copious ethnic menu and for the Spanish tradition of celebrating with families—with friends—and always with good food.

CIVIC CAFE

HARTFORD, CONNECTICUT

Located in what was once a bank facility in an office tower in downtown Hartford, the client—looking forward to an improving economy—decided to turn the 7,000 sq. ft. space into a restaurant "geared towards the business and professional sector of the city and the surrounding communities." A '90s urban cafe was proposed by the designer, Judd Brown, "to complement the eclectic and upscale menu."

The interior is an expansive volume which features original cast iron columns which are now clad in brushed aluminum sheathing. The same material appears on some of the walls adjacent to the bar. "The concept of metal juxtaposed against original refinished hard wood floors gives the urban-techy design look a very soft and warm appearance."

The two story high walls are finished in cherry stained particle board capped with black oak crown moldings. The moldings conceal the linear incandescent lighting, and above the black band the walls are glazed a honey yellow color "to depict the urban streetscape." The entire south wall of the building is decorated with a 65 ft. long mural of downtown Hartford done to resemble a charcoal sketch. Other areas of the wall surfacing carry giant graphics in cobalt blue that spell out "Civic." The word appears to be skewed on the wall and that adds "contemporary drama" to the space.

A main source of "theater" is the open kitchen and the movement that takes place in and out of it. Since light adds to the perception of drama, custom light fixtures were designed by the designer and made of brushed aluminum and perforated metal. They soften the lighting that emanates from the industrial-like chandeliers that shine through the custom light screens. In keeping with the "industrial" and "urban" concepts of the design, the furniture, fixtures and equipment were designed to continue the theme.

Bolt and washer details were used to secure the cushions to the booths and classic cafe seating, in light maple, was used with a palette limited to cobalt blue, silver and honey. The raised seating is covered in a classic tapestry to add a touch of drama to the eclectic environment, as does the striped marble floor.

The architect is currently preparing plans for a new second level "club facility" to be added onto this 250 seat restaurant.

DESIGN: *Judd Brown Designs, Warwick, RI*
PHOTOGRAPHER: *Warren Jagger, Providence, RI*

YELLOW GIRAFFE

The designer, Arthur de Mattos Casas, originally conceived this as an updated, "old-world cafe"; a small, quiet place to sit, relax, have a drink and watch the world go by outside—beyond the wide expanse of windows. What it is is a sleek, contemporary and smart, 1300 sq. ft. cafe with panache.

The facade is modern: crisp, clean and striking with black moldings separating the glazed areas and with stepped gray concrete panels below the windows. A small, black marquee extends out over the almost totally glass entrance doors and the name of the cafe is sandblasted on the glass transom panel. The designer also incorporated lighting into the black vertical uprights to either side of the doors and that same architectural motif is repeated inside the restaurant.

The interior floor is paved with miniature white ceramic glass tiles (vidrotil) accented with patterns in black squares. Important in the furniture and furnishing is the native Brazilian wood—Freijo—which was used in its rich, grained natural finish as well as ebonized for the chairs and table bases. The natural wood gleams on the backs of the chairs, on the table tops, across the bar that fills most of the rear of the space and also on the stairs, dividers and as accent trim on the black leather upholstered banquettes. The black columns and piers—with lighted elements—appear on the floor as well as on the back bar wall along with openwork grilles fashioned of the same, rich brown wood. The booths and the free standing chairs are also upholstered in the textured black leather.

DESIGN: *Casas Edicoes de Design, Sao Paulo, Brazil*
PHOTOGRAPHER: *Alain Brugier*

The walls are finished in a medley of pale creamy whites to almost golden yellow. The painted screen over the bar, by H.T., features the "Yellow Giraffes" amid prehistoric style wall "engravings" of animals executed in the "estuque" style. The color palette of the restaurant seems to emanate from this mural.

FEAST OF THE DRAGON

W. COLUMBUS, OHIO

Mark Pi is a household name in Ohio—especially if the household is tuned into Chinese cooking. Throughout the area, there are Mark Pi Express facilities in many malls and there is a two level one located in the Columbus Center which is presented in the Food Court/Fast Food chapter of this book.

Feast of the Dragon, designed by Frank Petruziello, for Mark Pi offers exotic Chinese gourmet cuisine in a buffet-style setting. The new operation is targeted at middle income families and the prototype, open kitchen, buffet restaurant is located in a 5,000 sq. ft. space.

The main design objective was to establish "a recognizable, repeatable identity" for the new chain. To accomplish this, the designer used "moveable icons" such as the buffet canopy, the entry pergola, the pagoda and the divider walls. "These elements can be rearranged to suit other space configurations yet maintain the desired identity." The open kitchen is visible from the entry and the buffet is located in front of the cooking line. A minimal sneeze guard was designed to allow viewing into the kitchen.

DESIGN: *Frank R. Petruziello, AIA*

Traditional Chinese themes are reinterpreted with new materials like a sunscreen net used for the roof of the pagoda. Bright colors are used for the furnishings, accessories and graphics—to provide a contemporary, family-oriented environment. Instead of installing a dropped, finished ceiling, the ceiling of the enclosure was painted black and flags are hung down from above—"enhancing the openness of the space and providing a festive atmosphere."

The small, colorful and high energy restaurant can seat 114 persons.

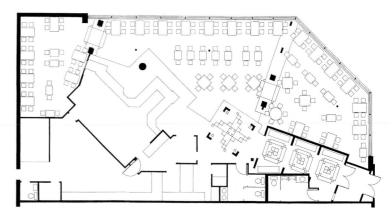

TERRA

GREENWICH, CONNECTICUT

Just as Frederick Brush Design Associates recreated the turn-of-the-century look in Le Figaro (also in this chapter), they have travel back in time—historically and architecturally—to design this attractive Italian restaurant called Terra. The goal was to achieve a "warm and romantic environment that is synonymous with the Tuscan influence of Northern Italy."

The ambience is a contrast of woods and stones—of natural materials in the colors of nature and the result is a warm and wonderfully relaxed dining experience in another time and place. The floor of the dining room has "the look of aged terrazzo that has been rediscovered." The design team has "aged" the tiles, chipped edges and in some cases broken them out. Where tiles are "missing" the "repair" is accomplished with assorted fragments of mismatched marble for a most unusual effect. In the front part of the restaurant where the angled bar is located, the lowered ceiling is patterned with wood beams and boards from which hang herbs, strings of garlic, peppers and an assortment of glowing copper cooking pans. A wood burning fire—just beyond the bar—lends its warmth to the dining area located back here.

DESIGN: *Frederick Brush Design Associates, Inc., Norwalk, CT*
  Frederick Brush
PROJECT MANAGER: *Kerry Gulick*
TECH. RESEARCH: *Kevin Ligos*
DRAFTSPERSON: *Ben Chanholm*
PHOTOGRAPHY: *Roy Wright Photography*

The ceiling of the dining room beyond consists of a series of vaulted bays which are illuminated by cove lighting. In the style of Titoretto these sky and cloud filled sweeps are filled with chubby cherubs or baroque style murals extolling the glories of food. In oval shaped rondels over the framed window murals, by Frederick Brush, the 18th-century motifs continue with painted foliage and swags. Framed graphics—like sepia sketches—look as though they were done by classic Italian artists and add to the "authenticity" of Terra.

Contemporary chairs and tables with "Euro-flair" provide the time travelers with an anchor in the present. "The look of the historic structure and the contemporary furnishings exist harmoniously to create a warm, inviting dining experience."

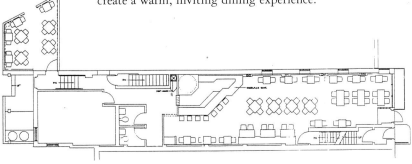

Food Courts
& Fast Foods

FOODLIFE, WATER TOWER PLACE, CHICAGO, ILLINOIS

FOODLIFE

"You have a social life, a business life, a family life and a love life. Now then, there is an environment dedicated to your food life." This is all about choices: at last a restaurant/food court which can seat 400 patrons and offer something for everybody—from a cup of coffee to a snack to a meal—at 12 stations where a variety of different types of healthy and healthful dishes are served.

The diner is invited into a verdant courtyard. As Martin Dorf, one of the principal designers of the themed stands describe it— "Foodlife was designed as an urban park fantasy and all of the food stands were conceived to showcase the preparation and display of food." Whether it is pizza, pasta, Asian specialties, or Mexican dishes—salads, soups, sandwiches, stuffed potatoes, burgers or baked goods—desserts, juices, coffee or tea—it is all here.

Dorf says, "A great deal of attention was focused on the food display to maximize the appeal of the variety of food offerings. Special custom made counters were constructed that tilt the food towards the customer's eye level. Special crockery, artifacts and decorative items were selected to complete the distinct personality of each food stand. Time-worn materials such as #2 pine were used to serve as a background for the color and drama of the food displays. The low voltage accent lighting enhances the freshness, color and appeal of the food."

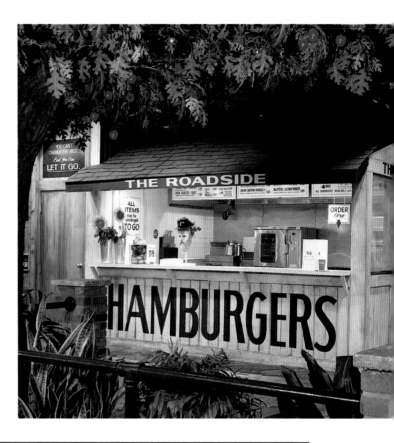

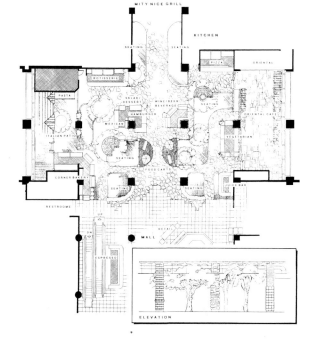

DESIGN: *Marv Cooper Design, Chicago, IL*
           Dorf Associates, New York, NY
PROJECT ARCHITECTS: *Jim Lencioni, Aria Group*
           Bill Aumiller, Aumiller Youngquist
DESIGN CONSULTANT: *Trudy Schwartz*
ARTISTS: *Paul Punke / Rick Neuhaus / Made in Chicago / Brian Sperry*
GENERAL CONTRACTOR: *Capitol Construction*
PHOTOGRAPHER: *Mark Ballogg, Steinkamp/Ballogg, Chicago, IL*

Foodlife, located in the 17,000 sq. ft. mezzanine of the vertical mall, Water Tower Place in Chicago, is another brilliant restaurant concept developed by Lettuce Entertain You's president, Rich Melman and his partner Steve Ottman. Marv Cooper, another of the designers of Foodlife says that "we (the design team) responded by creating a natural outdoor environment. We settled on the feeling of a park in a typical American small town where food vendors would converge on a festival weekend and set up stands." Diners are invited to meander along the path of "flagstones" to find clusters of food stands under boughs of foliage—not all visible at once, but "found" by turning with the snaking path. The designers created brick floored dining areas—like mini-picnic groves—furnished with outdoor cafe seating and rustic benches.

In creating the park-like ambience, American pine oak trees were formed from casts made of actual 18 in. to 24 in. diameter trees, and with a ceiling height of only 9 ft. 6 in., the diner never really sees the tops of the trees. The dark green ceiling is covered with drooping boughs of foliage and with the "neon-like track lighting" create a sense of unlimited height.

As previously stated, each stand has its own distinct personality and look. The Italian Kitchen is just that. Here pasta and pizza is available. Hamburgers can be purchased at the Roadside stand where they are freshly grilled. There is an earthy, down home look to Mother Earth's Grains. Martin Dorf who designed some of the stands says, "We wanted them to look authentic—as if they could actually exist."

Spit Roasted Chicken
SPECIALLY SEASONED WITH FOODLITES BLEND
OF SPICES HERBS and CITRUS JUICES and

ONE QUARTER BIRD   5.95
with two side dishes

ONE HALF BIRD   7.95
with two side dishes

ONE WHOLE BIRD   10.95
with two side dishes

Sides   1.25
• Vegetable of the day   • Pasta Salad
• Rice Pilaf   • Cous Cous
• Mashed Potato   • No fat Cole Slaw

Chicken Club Wrap

• White Meat Extra Charge

Cold Sides

MITY NICE GRILL   TABLE SERVIC

Sampling foods at Foodlife is no problem. Patrons are given a sensor card which can be "punched" at any of the stations. The diner can move freely—selecting from a variety of offerings and when the card is turned in at the cashier's desk it has a record of all of the purchases made. The patron pays only once: at the end of the gastronomic tour. According to Lettuce Entertain You, "This one stop payment system allows for convenient grazing."

As we become more conscientious about the environment and the world, we shall pass on to the future generation, the question of substance becomes global as well as personal. The Foodlife credo—"Be kind; eat true; it's now"—is our statement about how we feel about the world and our place in it. So be kind to the planet, eat what your body requires, and don't hesitate to be part of the solution. Now is the time to act if you want to make changes."

THE CAROUSEL FOOD COURT

WARWICK MALL

WARWICK, RHODE ISLAND

When it was decided that the Warwick Mall, the first major regional shopping center in Southern New England, required a major renovation—"to reestablish the center's 'identity'"—there was no question that a new food court would be essential to the redesign.

A new garden food court and entertainment center meant eliminating a junior department store and several small retail spaces but today a mall must be "an inviting destination for shoppers" and the mall management must find ways to keep the shopper on the site for extended periods—and that is what the food court can do. In keeping with Rhode Island's love for parks and gardens, an outdoor park concept became the unifying theme for Warwick Mall's new food court. It is "a cheerful, open space filled with natural light pouring in from multiple skylights." The natural light is further enhanced through the use of highly reflective, polished tile flooring.

The internally-lighted columns are covered with a green perforated metal—"to suggest the twinkle of lights through the branches of trees." In addition, there are light, colorful benches, chairs and tables, topiaries, trellises, a waterfall and for when the weather permits—an outdoor patio that can seat 100 patrons.

DESIGN: *Sumner Schein Architect, Cambridge, MA*

A new mall entrance permits direct access to the garden courtyard atmosphere of the food court where eleven tenants provide a varied selection of foods for the 500-seat space. "The interior graphics theme, neon lighting, and floor patterns are projected outside creating an urban style plaza whose centerpiece is an elevated, circular flower bed which is illuminated at night." A large scale video wall, the full size carousel, a game arcade and music and video stores all make the food court a place for week-long family entertainment.

In the first year of operation, the food court sales have more than covered the cost of the renovation and the foot traffic has had a two-fold increase.

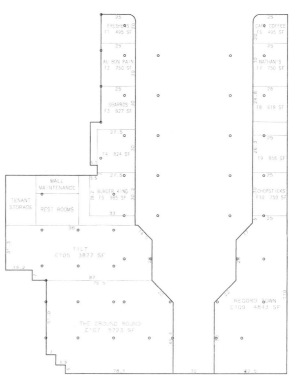

FOOD COURT, CAVENDISH MALL

ST. LUC, QUEBEC, CANADA

The Montreal design firm, Gervais/Harding Associates, was called upon to "cosmetically revamp" the existing Cavendish Mall in St. Luc. Working mainly with color and light, the designers were able to turn the dark, dreary and dull mall into something light, airy and as fresh as Springtime.

The new re-design called for not only a new ceiling and lighting system, but the introduction of the skylights which immediately brought daylight into the interior which was treated with a very light neutral palette by Faux et Uasage Faux. In addition, the new white tiled floors reflected more light back into the surroundings.

No where is the new open look more apparent than in the newly designed and installed food court where on the white textured ceramic tiled floors—accented in light blue—the gray metal chairs and tables are contrasted with the bright blue on the railing and the metal trim. A rich red color was also added to sparkle the otherwise neutral color scheme. Decorative trusses, painted with the same bright blue, were added in the center court. Trees in giant planters add to the park-like, outdoors feeling of the 400-seat food court. The decorative panel fascia over the in-line food stands and the uniform signs hanging at right angles out from the seven food concessions

DESIGN: *Gervais/Harding & Associates, Design, Inc., Montreal, Quebec*
ARCHITECTS: *Shapiro & Wolfe*
GENERAL CONTRACTOR: *Broccolini Construction, Inc.*
DECORATIVE METAL: *Carritec Inc., Serge Cantin*

Just beyond the food court—apart but still part of it—is the children's play area where the parents can still keep an eye of them—without leaving their food or coffee. The designers created a hulk of a pirate's ship where the children can climb, crawl or scamper—or just play "make believe." The flooring in this area is rubber tile.

THE FOOD FAIR

FOOD COURT, SOUTHLAND MALL

HAYWARD, CALIFORNIA

The objective for the T.L. Horton Design firm of Dallas was to create "immediate visibility," from the main level where all the retail action is located, down to the lower level where the food court is situated. "This was to become a new destination point for shoppers." Originally, the lower level was a truck tunnel and there was no visual contract between it and the retail level above.

The design firm created the logo and the name "Food Fair." Arched 16 ft. tall entries, located at the escalators leading down to the food area, were created to make the court visible. "A mobile, visible down mall corridor is made of 8 ft. foam, cut in shapes of food items, and it is suspended with aircraft wire from the 40 ft. ceiling." Not only did this make the food court visible throughout the mall but it satisfied Burger King's signage requirement which was necessary for them to sign the lease.

Also, a 16 ft. marquee with the Food Fair logo appears over the stage with the 150 ft. flowing red ribbon sculpted of sheet metal which decorates a long glass wall. The marquee is suspended with aircraft cable through the I-beams, and it defines the area for special events.

Directories are positioned on the main level and feature the names and locations of the food court tenants. In the court itself are banners and colored umbrellas added "for color and sound deflection."

DESIGN: *T.L. Horton Designs, Inc., Dallas, TX*
PHOTOGRAPHER: *Joe Aker, Aker Photography*

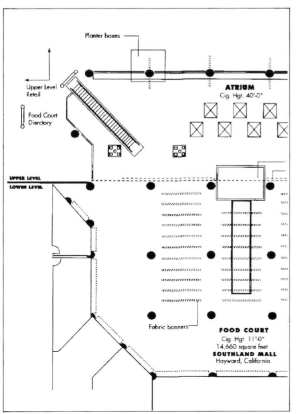

CAFES PANORAMA

BOULEVARD MALL

LAS VEGAS, NEVADA

In the midst of all the glitter, glitz and neon of Las Vegas there is an oasis of quiet and loveliness where the nickel that drops is not into a slot machine but onto the marble floor of the Boulevard Mall on Maryland Parkway—only a few blocks away from "the strip." This mall of over one million sq. ft. has been completely renovated by the RTKL Associates of Dallas.

In addition to four anchor stores—Sears, Penneys, Dillards and Broadway Southwest—there are 140 retailers in the light, airy, fountain and palm filled mall. Rather than "high rollers," the appeal here is to the families that live in and around Las Vegas—and to more families that are making Las Vegas a family vacation destination.
The architects' approach was to make the Boulevard "truly memorable." According to Tom Witt, V.P. in charge of design for RTKL, "We decided that what we couldn't fix—we would feature. We would build a new architectural theme around the very obstacles that we could not eliminate." The food court is a prime example of how this theory evolved in fact.

Within the long and narrow space prescribed for the Food Court, the architects "created a graceful, elliptical salon" with palm trees, fountains, and as a decorative feature to amuse and surround the diners—a 250 ft. x 8 ft. tall mural peopled with caricatures of famous stars and personalities of the "Golden Age" of the movies.

A frieze runs beneath the mural and it carries the famous "lines" spoken by the now immortals shown above. Located at the far end of the mall, the food court also serves to bridge the rest of the retail operations with the Sears department store that stands by itself beyond the court.

The food court, called Cafes Panorama, is warm and inviting; mostly in warm neutrals accented with black. The colors that are used on the logo design are used as accents throughout the space.

DESIGN: *RTKL Assoc., Dallas, TX*
PHOTOGRAPHER: *MMP/RVC*

ALTO LAS CONDES

FOOD COURT

SANTIAGO, CHILE

Completed only recently is the largest shopping center in Chile, the Alto Las Condes. It is located only a few miles away from downtown Santiago. Within the 850,000 sq. ft. space the designers built a three-level structure and provided for parking for over 3,000 autos. In addition to the 240 retail stores which includes two major department stores and a gigantic Jumbo Hypermarket, there is a food court which can accommodate 550 persons.

Though the oversized three story high columns are necessary for structural integrity, their overwhelming bulk has been minimized by dividing the columns midway. The upper portions are rounded like traditional columns but the lower halves are square block segments covered with beige and bronze colored marbles. The neutral colors help to soften the impact of the large scale dimensions.

A vaulted skylight runs the length of the building and almost all the interior surfaces are finished in a warm, off-white. Since the food court is located on the upper level of the mall, the space benefits from all the reflected light. The light background color was selected "to emphasize the brighter shades of the tenant's own color schemes and reinforce his individuality." Up on this level the protective railings are made of wood "to provide a soft and warm tactile sensation for passing hands." To further the up-scale image, the designers specified Argentinian granite for the floors.

DESIGN: *International Design Group, Toronto, Ontario, Canada*

The lighting plan in the food court includes PL ceiling fluorescent lamps in recessed fixtures. MR 16, low voltage lamps are used to "create a scalloped light effect—as well as a warmer tone to the edge of the bulkheads and the railings." Decorative seasonal banners, planters and foliage and clerestory windows all add to the fresh, clean feeling of the food court where the many tenants show up in stands filled with neon, ceramic tiles and bright, bright color.

PARQUE ARAUCO

FOOD COURT

SANTIAGO, CHILE

Located between downtown Santiago and the Alto Las Condes is the Parque Arauco which though older than the latter is still a fresh, viable and active mall. Interestingly, both malls—no more than 10 or 15 minutes from each other by car—are thriving and both have the same anchor department store and share many of the same name brand retail stores.

One reason for Parque Arauco's popularity as a destination is its active, energized and yet particularly restful food court which is located on the upper level. A huge, dome-like, glass and steel structure serves as the roof for the sitting area and here diners can relax under a sunny sky but enjoy it in an air-conditioned environment. It is as close as one can get to "al fresco" dining—or an outdoor cafe setting—without the negative factors like rain, heat, stinging sun rays or insects.

PHOTOGRAPHER: *MMP/RVC*

At the far end of the seating area—nearest the all-glass expanse is a raised stage—like a gazebo—where some of the black tables and gray marbleized laminate tables are highlighted with giant white canvas sun-brellas. The rest of the floor is tiled with off-white ceramic tiles accented with gray granite squares. A large ceiling vault extends over most of this food court but recessed under the shelves on either side are the many assorted food concessions. In the semi-darkness, the neon, the illuminated signage, and the bright reflective tiled counters stand out in bright colors. On the following page are some of the typical fast food stands found in the Parque Arauco.

PARQUE ARAUCO/
FAST FOOD STANDS

SANTIAGO, CHILE

Shown here are three typical examples of the food stands in the Parque Arauco food court. As in the United States, the menu is varied—it is international. Here, as in other malls everywhere, the diner can opt for Chinese, Japanese, Mexican, Italian or American style favorites along with typically native specialties.

Pagoda takes traditional Chinese architectural elements and adapts them to create a recognizable persona in the in-line counter space.

The scalloped green tile roof is supported by carved columns enriched with gilded entwining dragons touched with brilliant color. That facade says "Chinese" to any Chilean in search of egg rolls or any rice dish.

Chicken Inn—in name and style suggests an American—U.S.A. heritage. Many South Americans are attracted to things that say U.S. where it is in food or in clothes. The red/white and blue tile counter and the illuminated sign above the counter all restate the U.S.A. tradition as do the red neon bands that glow across the red painted background. All that's missing are the stars and stripes.

The rustic wood and the accent of red in the design of Le Parataga suggest a more country-casual or French provincial attitude. Here assorted crepes are made and served up. The biscuit colored tile floor blends with the natural, native wood planking used diagonally on the counter and the sign fascia above. The service counter and kitchen are somewhat recessed within the mall line—creating a degree of intimacy in the stand's design.

PHOTOGRAPHER: *MMP/RVC*

DESIGN: *Juan Carlos Lopez Studio, Buenos Aires, Argentina*
PHOTOGRAPHER: *Favio Balestrieri*

DE LO NUESTRO

GALERIAS PACIFICO

BUENOS AIRES, ARGENTINA

Located in the fast food area, on the lower level, is this striking fast food operation, De Lo Nuestro. In order to separate this operation from those surrounding it, the designers relied on a strong blue accent note to make their point.

For the design of the space gray and white ceramic tiles are combined in a strong checkerboard pattern. The pattern is repeated on the sweeping curve of the counter as well as on the rear wall in the service area. The on-view grilling and cooking is done in a triangular shaped projection at the far end of the space.

Here, too, the checkerboard pattern is lavishly used and natural wood is used as an accent and a buffer. According to the architects, "The idea of showing the client how and what is cooked—in front of their eyes—is a novelty—not a traditional view. "It is intended to eliminate "barriers between public and product." The showmanship plus the aroma of the barbecue makes De Lo Nuestro "brochettes"— a very popular item in this food court.

SKYLINE CHILI

COLUMBUS, OHIO

Skyline Chili, a long-time favorite in Cincinnati and its environs has decided to update and create a new visual image which would be strong enough to stand out from the competition in the new—and not so new—markets. FRCH, formerly SDI/HTI—a complete service store design/graphics house was called upon to design and prototype that new look.

This operation—a 2,400 sq.ft. space—was completely revamped in the new design which calls for "bold patterns—bright colors—and a slightly nostalgic" twist. It all begins on the outside where passing traffic would find it difficult not the see the blue and yellow checkerboard patter on the facade, the glisten and sparkle of the stainless steel trim and the sizzle of the red neon that streaks around the box-like structure. With more than a token bow to the roadside diners and truck strops along the major highways of the '50s, a giant sign beckons to the passing cars and trucks with a skyline logo oval above and a "streamlined checkered billboard base below.

Inside this fun, fast food space is also a return to the "diner days" of the '50s with the strong checkerboard pattern boldly taking over the floor and the front of the counter. Here, the color combination is red and yellow and it is accented with bright blue neon stripes. Glass blocks make a "return appearance behind the bar and "vintage" stools, upholstered in naugahyde, line up before the counter. Other authentic elements are "skillfully blended in a contemporary interpretation of a classic American diner" for today's relaxed and entertainment seeking patrons.

DESIGN: *FRCH, formerly SDI/HTI, NY*

COMITO'N'

FOOD COURT

ALTO LAS CONDES, SANTIAGO, CHILE

Comito'N is a large, self-serve, fast food operation located off in a corner of the Alto Las Condes food court. The bold red and white elliptical sign floats over the cream colored fascia and we are introduced to the warm, homey color feeling of the shop below. The cream and toast colors are repeated on the checkerboard patterned ceramic tile floor which is outlined with bands of a golden brown wood; the same wood that sheathes most of the interior walls, the counters, the booths on the side and the chairs and tables that are set out on a medium brown carpet in the center of the space.

Overhead the ceiling is turned into a grid with heavy timbers crisscrossing over the cream colored ceiling. Above the bar and the service counter in the rear, shingled wood canopies extend out over the counters to turn the setting into an open courtyard of a country ranch. The Ranchero imagery is enhanced by artifacts and decorative elements used on the shingled roofs, on the timber columns and on the shelves in the small bar located on the left side of Comito'N.

Up front a provincial wood table is laden with foods and gift items as well as rustic baskets piled up under the table. Throughout the space is warmly lit with incandescent lamps that are integrated into the ceiling timbers and the occasional drop lights. The open-for-viewing kitchen, behind the service counter—is contrasted by being lit with cool fluorescents.

PHOTOGRAPHER: *MMP/RVC*

MAX BEEF

AVENIDA FLORIDA, BUENOS AIRES, ARGENTINA

On the busy Avenida Florida, the main walking street in downtown Buenos Aires is one of the chain of hamburger stores called Max Beef. This is Argentina's answer to McDonald's and Burger King—both of which are represented nearby on this important shopping street.

Rather than a sleek, cool and contemporary look, the designers have taken their inspiration from more local and traditional sources. Not quite "rustica" or "ranchero"—but certainly not "big city." From the outside, Max Beef could be mistaken for a McDonald's—even to the "golden arch" that just happens to bow over the store's name in its logo design. Also, the red, yellow and white color scheme does seem familiar. Yet, as the customer approaches the largely fenestrated entrance, the space within is warm, rich, earthy, and much more Argentine in flavor.

Inside, the walls are covered with terra cotta tiles outlined with white grout for a pronounced, decorative grid pattern. Nowhere is this decorative quality more evident than in the series of open, see-through arches that visually connect the sitting space with the long service counter which lies beyond. The yellow from the logo is recalled in the pale curry color used on the wood edged, laminate topped tables and on the molded plastic seats. Black metal frames support the chairs and "float" the table top between them.

A deeper version of the logo red appears over the tiled arches. Incandescent lamps are used to softly illuminate the sitting area while fluorescents are added in the service counter space and in the mezzanine where additional seating is provided.

165

GREAT EATS FOOD COURT

GREAT MALL OF THE BAY AREA

MILPITAS, CALIFORNIA

Shoppers to the new mall in Milpitas enter through "The Great Train Court" where the theme and look for the mall is established. The floor is patterned like railroad tracks and "telegraph poles" are connected to each other with fiberoptic cables that light up to simulate electricity. The shopper is directed to a circular "Victorian Train Station" enclosed in plexiglass. An overhead platform—supported by columns—holds a model train that moves around a circular track. There are other devices and decorative elements employed like a ticket window, a large freight scale, chairs and sofas arranged to represent a first-class carriage of a century ago, and blasts of steam and an occasional sound of trains taking off or arriving.

In the Great Eats Food Court, the designers have skillfully blended elements relating to all forms of transportation in one highly animated environment." A ten-foot diameter globe, decorated with cars that light up, and planes, trains, and ships that circle around it,

hangs over the information desk at the entrance. Overhead—in the center of the court is a series of eight postcards arranged in a star pattern that rotates around the central column. Nostalgic scenes of "romantic old California" appear on these overscaled postcards. Hanging from them are strings of small lights in various shapes relating to food and travel.

The table tops in the food court have collages embedded in them of maps, postcards, and photos of olden days of travel. The food retailers' storefronts feature giant roadside billboards that call out to the prospective diners. A giant silhouette that completely circles the food court—beyond and above the shopfronts—depicts a continuous horizon that goes from a rural landscape to a city skyline. The mural is back lit and glows like "a distant skyline glimpsed by travelers late at night." A giant 1950-ish sign with the food court's logo stands outside of the entrance.

DESIGN: *FRCH, formerly SDI/HTI*

MGM "BACKLOT" FOOD AREA

MGM GRAND

LAS VEGAS, NEVADA

Standing on a valuable, one square mile tract of land in Las Vegas, off the famous Las Vegas Blvd. is the MGM Grand Hotel — and grand it is indeed! The big, sprawling, multi-faceted and multi-leveled building rises up like all of Oz from the flatness that surrounds it. Behind it is the MGM Backlot theme park where visitors can "travel" all around the world and back again in a fanciful and romanticized version of architecture and geography according to the artists of Disney.

Visitors are free to wander down "stage sets" and enjoy the man-made vistas—meander along crooked lanes "centuries" old—cross over bridges—and there are "photo-ops" all along the way. Enhancing the world tour that goes from the streets of Little Old N.Y. with its brownstone/stoop buildings and an "el" train running overhead—through a sleepy Tudor-style English village—into the remnants of a wild west town—to a street in New Amsterdam mirrored in a canal—to the wharf of a city on the Mississippi River with a paddle boat steamer lined up next to it—through the architectural vignettes of Germany, France, Italy and a series of exotic Asian ports—enhancing all of this are the fast food operations that are designed to blend in with the surroundings.

PHOTOGRAPHER: *MMP/RVC*

In old England, behind the half-timber facade of stucco, wood and stone is a Burger King. A pizzeria is located in an Italian Tyrol building full of fanciful, decorative trims, flower boxes, and plantings. In the slate paved courtyard, up front, curved benches and round tables with red/white/green umbrellas invite the "time travelers" to rest awhile and enjoy the "local" treats. Nathan's Deli has been transported and situated in a recreated New Orleans structure enriched with curlicue grillwork, colorful shutters, arcades and plants. This building is just across the road from the Cotton Blossom paddleboat that is anchored in an artificial lagoon.

In a brick building that would have been comfortable in Concord when Paul Revere went off on his midnight ride is a Kenny Rogers operation where his Roasters are available to today's minutemen and women—and their kids. A Mexican piazza with its Jesuit architecture church beyond is the setting for the Rio Grande Cantina where the Mexican specialties are available.

The pagoda-like structure in the Asian area features a varied menu of Chinese, Japanese and Thai foods and the architectural elements reflect many of the same Asian cultures. Back, at last, in Old New York, the visitor can pull up to an old trolley car that now sells simple U.S.A. specialties in a handsomely recreated, nostalgic setting.

And—not once do you hear the jingle-jangle of the coins dropping into the slots!

MARK PI'S EXPRESS

CITY CENTER MALL

COLUMBUS, OHIO

Located in the heart of downtown Columbus, OH is the new, multi-leveled urban mall—the City Center Mall. Not only is this a shopping center, but the food court takes on an even greater importance as an "oasis" or "watering hole" for the shoppers as well as the office workers in the many high rise office buildings that surround the mall. One of the more popular destinations here is Mark Pi's Express. The Mark Pi operation, in Ohio, is a well known and respected phenomenon where Chinese cooking is in demand.

Mark Pi's goal is to offer "Imperial Chinese cuisine with the convenience of fast preparation and lower prices." Important in all of the Mark Pi outlets is the open kitchen. It is important so that the customers can see the "drama of Chinese cooking." "Patrons are witness to the spectacular display of flames emanating from the wok as the chef prepares their meals which usually takes less than 60 seconds."

The main objective, in this location, was to design a fast food restaurant in which the cooking area was at the store front line and yet leave enough room for seating within a 20 ft. wide space. The architect/designer, Frank Petruzielli, narrowed the Express cooking/serving line to approximately 10 ft. so that tables could be accommodated.

DESIGN: *Frank R. Petruziello, AIA*
PHOTOGRAPHER: *Peter Megert*

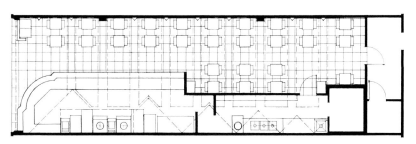

To create a feeling of space, a half arched ceiling was installed and the other half is reflected in a mirrored wall on the opposite side. The kitchen wall was kept low so that the curved metal panels could extend overhead enhancing the feeling of width in the space. Indirect lighting of the metal panels also tends to accentuate the height of the room—"adding to the feeling of openness." The overall store space is 1,500 sq. ft.: 20 ft. wide x 75 ft. long.

FLYING WEDGE PIZZA

CAMBIE ST., VANCOUVER, BC, CANADA

Fun and imagination go into a Flying Wedge Pizza along with the wonderful, healthy and sometimes unexpected ingredients.

From the facade out on the street into the small but cleverly conceived shops (only 700 sq. ft. for Cambie St.), Flying Wedge Pizza is a treat and a graphic delight. Even reading the menu is part of the entertainment here: Beauty and the Beef, Cornan the Bavarian, Popeye, The Big Yum, Broken Hearts, Hot Licks, Veggie Wedgie, etc.

This new store opened in what was previously a travel agency and the floor plan, according to the owner, entrepreneur, designer—Harvey Chiang—resembled a "triangular pie shape" with the widest portion being the storefront. This wedge shape reduced the kitchen area to a narrow point making everything inside the store "look smaller and compressed." To overcome this, the designer combined strong visual shapes such as wedges, angles and even a rocket ship—along with vibrant colors—to draw attention away from the small, cramped space. Instead of the usual bulky heat lamps that hang over counters, the designer conceived custom "rocket ship" housings for the heat lamps—to add another decorative note to the design while reinforcing the space-y theme.

DESIGN/CONSTRUCTION: *H. Chiang Enterprises*
PHOTOGRAPHER: *Stuart Dee Photography*

"Boulders tumbling out of a stream of stainless steel panels" also help to create a "visual field" to mask the otherwise bulky service counter. Also, the signage, graphics, furniture and furnishings are all cleverly detailed and customized to add to the out-of-this-world attitude of Flying Wedge Pizza.

An interesting note: There is a 25 cent rebate to customers who bring in their own container or re-use one they already have. This is the effort of Harvey Chiang to run an enviro-friendly fast food operation. "We ask people to take personal action in reducing waste: This requires a subtle change in lifestyle and a greater one in mentality but it is a request we feel will seem increasingly reasonable." That message is printed on the back of the company's menu.

PECOS BILL'S RESTAURANT

This food court restaurant is basically a "barbecue stand" designed "to evoke image of roadside barbeque eateries in Texas."

A larger-than-life "Peco's Bill"—outlined in neon—stands up front to direct the customers into the "sit-down" restaurant. The barn-shaped entrance is framed in a blue metal truss with a corrugated roof which extends into the restaurant where it overhangs the service/order area. Rustic materials are used throughout to contrast with the modern feeling of the surrounding mall. Barbecued meats and grill items are presented in the order area where they are prepared and sliced in front of the customer. On the curved, low wall of sandstone, near the order area, are large black kettles filled with chili for ladling and other assorted sauces the diners can spoon over their orders. Large TV monitors display menu items and prices as well as pictures while, on other TV monitors, the patrons can relax—feel at home—and be entertained by country-western music videos.

In the sitting area there are deep stained, wood booths lined up along the walls and tables and chairs are grouped in the center. Within the deeply-recessed niches on the walls there are Texas related memorabilia such as road maps, license plates, sign posts, flags, posters and—of course—longhorn steer skulls. The center of the dining room is covered by a large Texas Lone Star flag, painted on gypsum board with clouds, and sky painted in the cut-out portion of the single star in the flag.

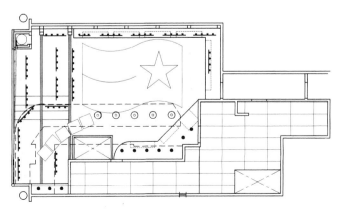

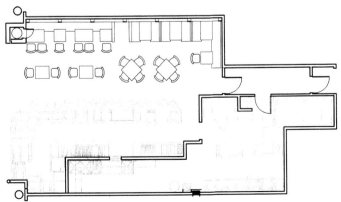

ARCHITECT/DESIGNER: *61st Place Architects, Scottsdale, AZ*
PHOTOGRAPHER: *Rafique Islam*

SOUPER SALADS

MESA, ARIZONA

Though this Souper Salad is, in many ways, adapted from the prototype shown in Book 3 of this series, there were changes made to adapt the design to the peripheral parcel around a regional mall. In this case, the entrance is located in the corner of a covered walkway.

The main dining room has a high ceiling which contributes to the overall feeling of light and spaciousness. Brightly colored curved elements appear on the ceiling over the soup and salad bars which are the main distribution areas in this design and, as in the previous design, bright posters adorn the back wall behind the salad bar. A "soupergraphic" wall covering extends behind the soup bar for extra interest and color.

In the seating area there is a colorful floral carpet on the floor and pendant downlights are hung over each dining group. The general illumination in the restaurant is supplemented by indirect uplights located in the soffits above the soup and salad bars. The two bars are also illuminated—for special attention—by color corrected spots— "to draw attention to the true color and texture of the food display."

DESIGN: *61st Place Architects, Scottsdale, AZ*
PHOTOGRAPHER: *Rafique Islam*

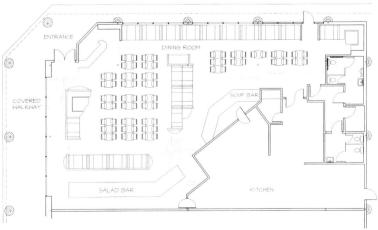

KFC EXPRESS!

PROTOTYPE DESIGN

KFC Express! is a new prototype design created by Design Forum for the Kentucky Fried Chicken company for a "quick serve food station featuring snackable KFC menu items." The format is intended to capture customers in "non traditional locations." The 10 ft. x 10 ft. miniaturized cooking platform is flexible enough to be applied as a kiosk in an airport or transportation center as well as an in-line or counter top display for corporate, university or hospital cafeteria facilities.

To reinforce the "brand equity of the Colonel's original restaurants," the brightly colored and eye-arresting "KFC Express!" logo was conceived by Design Forum's graphic artists. "An angled white cube, bright accents in a primary color scheme, combined with illuminated pictorials provide excitement and energy at each location."

The graphics and design elements are also extended into the product packaging and presentation in the kiosk/stand.

DESIGN: *Design Forum, Dayton, OH*
Bill Chidley, V.P. of Design
Carolyn Zudell, Creative Director & Graphic Design

DESIGN: *GGLO Architects & Int. Design Group, Seattle, WA*
PHOTOGRAPHER: *Yannis Patrzarisos*

BRUEGGER'S BAGEL BAKERY

SEATTLE, WASHINGTON

Bruegger's Bagel Bakery is the first of the 20 bakery/delicatessen outlets being planned for Western Washington by the franchisee, Pacific Capital Ventures. The architectural design firm, GGLO, worked with the operator to establish a "regional standard by modifying and adapting existing requirements to be more appropriate to the proposed locations and operator's preferences."

A display baking area features the activity of the bagel oven and kettle—and the ongoing process of making bagels. The designers took advantage of the high ceiling, exposed it, and increased the visibility of the space. In addition, the ceiling was opened to allow daylight in through a new divided light transom glazing. A rich, bright blue curved valance sweeps out over the curved counter below and it carries—way over eye level—the Bruegger's logo.

Another blue fascia, not as deep, follows the undulating, white tiled counter decorated with a checkerboard pattern in blue. The counter is topped in gray. The white wall behind the counter carries assorted blue and white sign boards. The blue soffit, mentioned, disguises the HVAC system needed to ventilate the bagel ovens.

Off-white ceramic tiles are used on the floor and the white laminate table tops sit on dark blue bases. The natural maple wood, bentwood style, chairs are light in color and the same maple is used for accents, trims and moldings in the store. The customer areas are effectively lit with pendant and track lighting. A soft canvas banner, spattered with gold, blue and red stars—like the fascia over the counter—swags down from the ceilings and as it swoops back—it leads the diners to the rear of the long space.

MARKETS,
FOOD STORES
&
SPECIALITY
SHOPS

DEAN & DELUCA MARKET

GEORGETOWN, WASHINGTON, DC

Paris has its Fauchon, Milan has its Salumeria Montenapoleone, London has its Harrod's Food Hall, and New York has its Dean & Deluca. Now, Washington, DC can also boast of its very own Dean & Deluca Market in its midst.

When the groumet market decided to open in the Capitol area, they opted for a Markethouse built in 1802 in the historic Georgetown section and when the company selected Core of Washington to redesign the space—the mission was evident. "The store must appear as though it's been here for a hundred years—no one should know that we (the designers) have been here." Since the building has great historical significance, special care was taken to incorporate the technically complex program required to make a functioning, state-of-the-art market.

The new standing seam roof matches the original, but also accommodates the complicated mechanical and exhaust needs of the new market. The floor "floats" free and unattached to the walls while beneath it are thousands of feet of concealed conduit and piping to the assorted equipment. This preserves the existing historic structure—"controlling the location and form of all exposed utility services creates a harmony within the existing rhythm of the structure."

A canopy structure, attached to the exterior, created an outdoors cafe area. Except for that, the only other exterior changes were minor renovations and the repainting of the trim and doors. According to the designers, "function and place combine to create a unique space" and here, within the shell, they have affected an exciting place for the display of foods and the wares—and that "provides the life, vitality and interest necessary for the atmosphere of successful retail."

This Marketplace not only won an award for "Historic Resources" but also one for the "retail interior" design.

DESIGN: *Core, Washington, DC*
    Robert D. Fox, AIA / Peter F. Hapstack III, AIA / Dale A. Stewart, AIA
FORDEAN & DELUCA: *Design: Jack Ceglic*
PHOTOGRAPHER: *Michael Moran*

CORRADO MARKET

NEW YORK, NY

The Corrado family has made a reputation for itself in NYC. It started with the Corrado restaurant in midtown Manhattan where Jack Baum, of Tree House Design, first had contact with the family.

This was followed by the successful Corrado Kitchen which is a gourmet take-out/food store where many of the pasta dishes prepared in the restaurant are offered along with staples like sandwiches, pastries and coffee. The "Kitchen" is conveniently located in an storefront adjacent to the restaurant and has recently doubled in size and now has a small open display kitchen which is a visual attraction.

The Corrado Market is located in a more residential, upper East Side neighborhood and follows the family's expansion into Corrado Cafe which recently opened in the same area. The Market is a complete "grocery store" offering—in addition to what is offered in Corrado Kitchen—a complete line of gourmet specialty products.

The low suspended acoustic tile ceiling was removed and a new ceiling was applied directly on to the store's rafters. The space takes on a feeling of greater height and the now-exposed plumbing lines and visible ducts create a sort of functional, warehouse atmosphere.

The walls were stripped to the brick and left bare while unfinished pine planks with exposed nails are used for the shelving in the store. Large ceramic tiles are used on the floor throughout the space.

Corrado Market has its own kitchen which is designed to be seen by

the public. It was made visible to "reinforce the knowledge that all the food is fresh and prepared on the premises." The kitchen is located at the rear of the long, narrow space; a typical Manhattan store layout. The cooking area is highlighted with the flourescent lighting scheme that contrast with the front of the store which is illuminated with warm, incandescent pendant lighting fixtures. "This helps to draw the customers' attention when they enter the store," and entices them to travel through the entire length of the store—exposing them to all the beautifully prepared and presented food offerings. All the refrigerated cases are state-of-the-art, Italian cases with maximum glass areas which contrast with the otherwise "rustic" and "factory" setting.

In addition to the open kitchen and produce department, Corrado Market has a separate coffee and dessert bar, a vast selection of coffee beans and a dairy area.

DESIGN: *Tree House Design, New York, NY*
Julius S. Baum
PHOTOGRAPHER: *Stephen Carr, New York, NY*

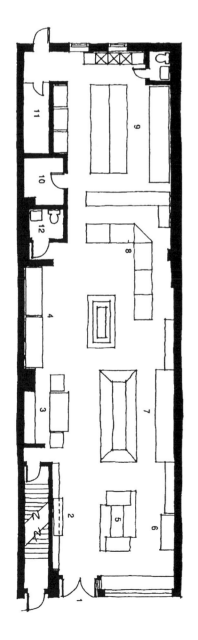

FOODLIFE MARKET

WATER TOWER PLACE, CHICAGO, ILLINOIS

Foodlife Market is located in the Foodlife food court (reviewed in the chapter on Food Courts) on the mezzanine level of Water Tower Place in Chicago. Martin Dorf of Dorf Associates in NYC worked with Marv Cooper of Chicago on the design of the whole Foodlife area and Dorf conceived this market as a place to get "delectable, fresh, prepared foods"—to eat in or take out. The selections offered in the market include both hot and cold dishes presented in a self-service format and the emphasis in the food preparation is on healthy, low-fat, organic ingredients.

The space was created to be part of the total food court design and yet stand apart as an entity. The brightly lit entrance display "focuses attention on the abundantly displayed packaged goods" with fresh produce and other offerings visible beyond. Baskets are mounded with product display and from overhead there is a downpouring of cooking utensils, salamis, cheeses, and many more rustic woven baskets in assorted shapes and sizes—"all contributing to the market atmosphere" that extends throughout the space.

The shopper can wander over to the prepared foods stand where, in seamless glass cases, there is a tempting display of hot and cold prepared dishes. Packaged snacks are piled up in wicker and rattan baskets and panniers on the floor in front of the cases. Through an arched window, the patron can see into the food preparation area—"contributing a sense of activity and freshness to the presentation."

Also, there is a salad bar—tilted towards the patron—and the colorfully presented produce above "visually reinforces the image of freshness and quality." Sandwiches are artfully arranged and wrapped in clear cellophane and stacked at an angle to make the selection process simpler. Fresh breads and desserts—in their own area—are also available in the Foodlife Market.

DESIGN: *Dorf Associates, New York, NY*
Martin Dorf
ARCHITECT: *Walter Panncewicz, ARIA Group, Oak Park, IL*
FOOD SERVICE DESIGN: *Beth Kuczera, Boelter Co., Lincolnwood, IL*

SALUMERIA MONTENAPOLEONE

Via Montenapoleone, Milan, Italy

Say "Via Montenapoleone" and to the fashion cognoscenti it means "high fashion—Milan style." Say it to a gourmet of fabulous foods and the answer will be "the Salumeria"—the unbelievable marble, glass and brass delicatessen store located amidst Krizia, Mila Schoen, Dior and Versace. Located on this upper-upper crust fashion street in the heart of Milan's upwardly mobile fashion area is this gilded grocery with the trappings and details of a bygone era.

The wealth and richness of the produce, provisions and provolones are evident at once in the illuminated display windows that also afford a view into the fabulous merchandising within. Everything here is artfully and tastefully displayed: presented to maximize the visual appeal to the senses. Colors and textures of the foods are enhanced by the colors and textures that surround them. Throughout—in the windows as well as in the interior—square, pressed glass shades—like crystal—on gleaming brass stems provide the warm, flattering light to the foods and the ambient materials. The raised ceiling elements are illuminated by hidden fluorescents.

Deep brown woods and veneers are used to add to the elegant, upscaled look of the space as are the gray-green, hand fashioned shaped tiles which are accented with bands of olive green and black granite. Along with the shine of the brass there are long stretches of satin, stainless steel highlighting the handsome, glass fronted display cases. The prepared foods and provisions are presented on simple white dishes and bowls to complement the colors of the edibles. Hanging cheeses, salamis, and dried meats are used decoratively as are the copper and brass cooking utensils and rustic baskets. On the shelves that line the walls behind the serving counter and in the niches there are jars and bottles and oversized glass presentation containers filled with fanciful patterns of pickled mushrooms, peppers and olives of all shades and tints stuffed with myriad relishes.

PHOTOGRAPHER: *MMP/RVC*

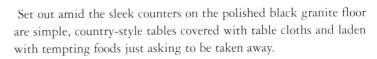
Set out amid the sleek counters on the polished black granite floor are simple, country-style tables covered with table cloths and laden with tempting foods just asking to be taken away.

OLD FRENCH MARKET

FRENCH QUARTER, NEW ORLEANS, LOUISIANNA

Farmers' Markets are becoming more and more a part of the urban scene and lifestyle. The "olden days" are being revived in the centers of cities and farmers are once again bringing their fresh produce—fruits, vegetables, freshly baked pies and breads, flowers and staples—for the city folk to pleasure in. In NYC, old Union Square is alive two times each week with the sights, smells and sounds of farmers hawking their wares at colorful stands surrounded by skyscrapers and structures of cold steel and glass.

The Old French Market in the French Quarter of New Orleans is a "must see—must stop—must shop" spot highlighted on any walking tour of the historic area. In a centuries old structure—a long arcade with a pitched timber roof and sides open to the charming, colorful surroundings—there are dozens of open stands set into the arched openings. The wares—in baskets, bushels and wooden boxes—tumble forward into and onto the crowded concrete aisle which is always filled with gaping tourists and knowing natives.

In amid the fruits and vegetables there are stands with local "specialties" intriguingly packaged and ready to travel with the tourist who wants to bring back tangible memories of the Creole and Cajun cuisines of New Orleans. Herbs and spices abound as do prepared mixes for many "local" dishes. There are stands with fresh foods "to go" and there is even a fully stocked and equipped fish market that is almost a shop unto itself.

PHOTOGRAPHER: *MMP/RVC*

All that makes a Farmer's Market such a pleasure and treat are here: the sights, smells, and tastes plus the ambience that is at once traditional—yet exotic for "city folk." It is difficult to resist the outpouring from the unending cornucopia of fresh produce and unusual products as well as the neat, organized presentation of packaged goods in tempting, try-me, displays.

LONSDALE MARKET

LONSDALE QUAY

W. VANCOUVER, BC, CANADA

The lower level of this two story high corrugated aluminum, steel, glass and concrete barn-like structure is devoted to Lonsdale Market, a Farmer's Market on the water's edge. The people who live in West Vancouver find this an ideal place to shop for fresh fruits, vegetables, baked goods, meats, fish, cheese, etc., and also an unending selection of prepared "ethnic" foods—or the makings for exotic or gourmet repasts. For those who travel to or from work by ferry—this market which is only a minute or two from the ferry landing—is an ideal place to put together a "quick" meal or the fixings for a feast.

The open center area of the "festival" building is an atrium into which sunlight streams down from the overhead skylights—aided and abetted by the pendant halogen lamps to dispel and gray or gloom.

The stands are interspersed with kiosks on the concrete floor and the perimeter walls are lined with specialty "stores" or prepared food operations where you can "take-out" or "eat-in" in a sitting area provided beyond the selling floor. Bright seasonal banners hang overhead and some of the stands and counters add their own special pizzazz with canvas awnings and tent tops.

PHOTOGRAPHER: *MMP/RVC*

DUSO'S ITALIAN MARKET

LONSDALE QUAY

W. VANCOUVER, BC, CANADA

Typical of the shops and stands is Duso's Italian Market which is centrally located in the atrium and somewhat dominates the space by its size and the variety of products displayed. Here, too, the shopper can select from pastas, cheeses, salamis, sausages, sauces and such to fill prepared dishes ready to travel and be reheated at home. The Italian colors—red, white, green—are prominently displayed and then integrated into the space as well as props and textures that we think of as "Italiano Rustica." Though it is out in the open, the design is enveloping and manages to create a distinct feeling and ambience for Duso's—and the products being offered.

PHOTOGRAPHER: *MMP/RVC*

FAREPLAY

Although Statoil is a state-owned oil company of Norway, the company recently acquired some of the British Petroleum sites in Ireland. CDI Group, Inc. was asked to develop a "state of the art" facility for these new Irish Statoil outlets.

The convenience store/market prototype was created in a space of under 1,000 sq.ft. The exterior design uses a dramatic architectural treatment to highlight the store's entrance which is further enhanced by the triangular logo which, in effect, points to the way to the entrance. The red, orange and white color scheme is introduced out here. The designers still maintained "the integrity of existing corporate identity standards."

DESIGN: *CDI Group, Inc, Riverdale, NY*
Project Principal/Designer: Joseph M. Bona
Project Manager: Anthony Coll
Graphic Designer: Denise Guerra
CLIENT: *Statoil, Ireland*
PHOTOGRAPHER: *Statoil, in house*

Inside the convenience shop, the shoppers follow "an induced traffic pattern" which leads them to and past the freshly baked goods and the beverages. It was the design firm's intention to combine the store's layout, the colors, and the signage 'to create a strong first impression" and also to expose the shopper to the full range of high margin, impulse products and services. Photographic images are used here for decoration as well as information. The rich, full-color photo-graphs and the vibrant graphics designed for Fareplay "create visual excitement"—while maintaining the differentiation of planned purchase categories and impulse food service items.

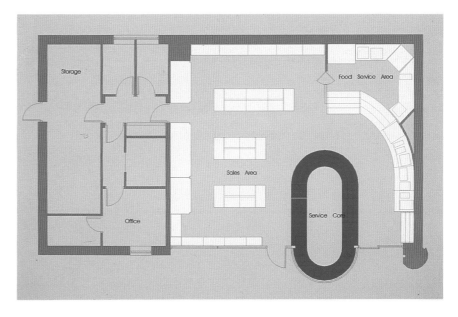

LA COCINA

For this mall, fast food operation, the design firm, Juan Carlos Lopez Studio, returned to the "past" and "revived" in contemporary terms, the romantic attitude towards the old kitchens that appeared in the "estancias" on the southern Pampas of Argentina. Based on materials and imagery typical of the old kitchens in haciendas, the designers faced the rear wall of the space with old brick and used native materials, unfinished woods for show counters, cases and shelves. In the glass enclosed but open-for-viewing kitchen ceramic tiles are combined with gleaming copper and marble topped work counters. The glass display shelves that stand atop the marble topped service/display counter are supported by copper tube uprights and illuminated by the lamps in the dropped metal shades. The store's signage is a back-lit, sand blasted glass panel with applied letters.

DESIGN: *Juan Carlos Lopez Studio, Buenos Aires, Argentina*
PHOTOGRAPHER: *Favio Balestrieri*

VALENTI

Located in the award winning Patio Bullrich is Valenti, a truly upscaled and very exclusive specialty food store. It is on the second level and only steps away from the food court. The shop is almost totally on view through the wide windows that flank the dramatic entrance into the shop. The windows are not only filled with exquisite food beautifully illuminated, but they also frame the very handsome interior.

The limestone facade is trimmed with brushed brass and accented with deep red. The brass and limestone/marble continues inside the store as well. Valenti belongs to an old, well known Argentine family, of Italian origin, and has made its reputation with the manufacture and sale of gourmet cheeses and delicatessen. In keeping with the 19th century heritage of Patio Bullrich and the long time legacy of the Valenti name, the designers of the mall also designed this shop with a "distinctive and aristocratic" look. The excellent lighting inside the store, as in the window display area, plus the opulent setting, all enhance the product display.

DESIGN: *Juan Carlos Lopez y Assoc., Buenos Aires, Argentina*
PHOTOGRAPHER: *Favio Balestrieri*

DOLCI E DOLCE

VIA VITTORIO EMANUEL, MILAN, ITALY

Just a few streets down from the Duomo and the handsome old Vittorio Emanuel shopping arcade and on the noted shopping street one can find Dolci e Dolce tucked away under one of the classic arcades. The tiny marble and wood lined shop serves only as the background for the fabulous display of candy, cookies and gelati.

The single, open backed window is filled with angled metal shelves that each carry their own fluorescent lamps to light up the products on show below. In addition to the torrone, the cotognata and the miraculous collection of marzipan fruits and vegetables, there are also assorted cookies and nut and honey treats.

Inside, the narrow store has glass showcases lined up along all of the right side wall. The gelati is presented in the first refrigerated case—upon entering—next to the wide, plate glass door.

The walnut wood facing on the cases is complemented by the whitish marble base and the band of stainless steel that streaks down the length of the cases. The wall behind the counter is clad in walnut veneer with arched pediments over the recessed shelves where gift packages are shown. Between the arched "bookcase" units is a wide panel of mirror. The wall opposite the counters is also mirrored to "open" up the space.

Squares of dark gray marble pattern the floor and overhead the ceiling is raised in an elliptical design. The central raised area is washed by hidden fluorescent tubes behind the cove and incandescent spots are set into the raised ceiling which also makes a decorative element out of the HVAC vents. The rear wall of the store also is sheathed with a panel of smoked mirror.

PETAK'S

UPPER MADISON AVE., NEW YORK, NY

The market has changed! The area has changed: the trade has changed and Petak's realized that if it wanted its share of this new, upwardly mobile market it would have to change its appeal and look—if not its product which is still very desirable. The store was originally conceived as "an assembly line" where customers could line up in the 25 ft. x 75 ft. store to place their orders—see it "manufactured" and move on down to pay for it. Meanwhile, in a space of almost the same size—1,700 sq. ft.—in the basement kitchen a crew of cooks and bakers prepared the foods and baked goods sold up on the street level. The original store was a jumble of counters—of corners—of areas of merchandise tucked away—and shoppers had to move from area to area looking for and hopefully finding what was wanted.

Today, the 11 cooks and four bakers prepare a menu of over 80 upscale entrees and salads that cater to the taste of the community. This part of Madison Ave. is now the home to a variety of museums and fashionable, fashion stores and according to Mr. Patak—"They are pleased to use the neighborhood more and want a place to come in and sit down." The new Petak's has been redesigned by Natan Bibliowicz and it satisfies the client's desire to satisfy the "new marketing priorities.

DESIGN: *Natan Bibliowicz Architects, P.C., New York, NY*
Natan Bibliowicz, Principal in Charge
Design: Fiona McCarthy
Technical: David Light

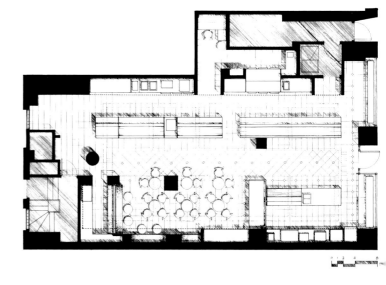

The new facade is more in keeping with the clientele of this "Carnegie Hall" neighborhood. Granite faces parts of the facade and a boxy new green awning with logo spans across the shop's front. Inside the changes are even more profound. Gone are the gourmet packaged foods since local grocery stores are carrying the same products and at comparable prices. More attention has been given to the baked goods and the prepared foods—and space has been allotted for patrons to sit and enjoy a cup of coffee—a quick repast—or just wait for service. The floor is covered with reddish terra cotta tiles and the walls are curry colored accented with a deep yellowish green. These same colors appear on the coved ceiling, the recessed wall areas and in the yellow colored tiles behind the service area and the glass counters in the prepared foods area.

The serving line takes up most of the right hand side of the store and the shopper can make selections from the easily viewed foods in the curved glass fronted cases. A small espresso/coffee bar is located opposite the far end of the service line. The bar is finished with crackled glass and a copper sheet base and trim. A series of stools with black "coiled spring" bases are topped with green upholstered seats and there are some granite topped tables set out, with the Jacobsen chairs.

The space is illuminated by low voltage MR16s secured to nearly invisible wires stretched across the three raised ceiling openings over the service line on the right, and the green cove conceals additional lights. Other light fixtures have been placed in the central green ceiling strip. Accenting the placement of these lamps are the decorative tiles set into the terra cotta floor beneath them.

Acting as his own contractor, Mr. Petak—working with the architect/designer—was able to bring about this startling metamorphosis for $175,000.

SNAK WORKS

ONTARIO, CANADA

Surprisingly, Canadian Tire Petroleum is Canada's largest retailer and they have particular strength in the sale of automotive, leisure and home products. More than 50 percent of their outlets feature "gas bars": sell fuel. Snak Works was designed as a convenience store/market to go with these gas pumping stations.

"The objective of the design program was to create a retail identity that was separate from but related and equal to the Company's large-scale retail outlets." The prototype design is only 800 sq.ft. The store structures are pre-fabricated and shopped to the site by trailer—"thus minimizing field construction and optimizing both cost and quality control." The interior design is driven by the strong graphics program created for Snak Works by the design firm. Photomurals are featured to promote the high margin prepared foods available, and also the self-serve beverage department. To maximize the effectiveness of the merchandising in the small space, a highly disciplined and controlled signage program was installed.

DESIGN: *CDI Group, Inc., Riverdale, NY*
Project Principal: Gerald Lewis
Project Manager/Design: Nanette Gran
Graphic Designer: Denise Guerra
Client: Canadian Tire Petroleum
PHOTOGRAPHER: *Canadian Tire Petroleum, in house*

PACIFIC MARKETPLACE

DESIGN: *Sunderland Innerspace Design, Vancouver, BC Canada*
Jon Sunderland

NORTHWEST PASSAGE

SEATTLE-TACOMA INTERNATIONAL AIRPORT, WASHINGTON

Northwest Passage is a unique setting of stores in the Seattle/Tacoma International Airport where travelers can find "souvenirs" of many kinds to bring home. Of special interest is the Pacific Marketplace and the Liar's Seafood shops.

The Marketplace takes up 1,170 sq. ft. and is dedicated to merchandising regional foods. "The concept of this area, is a subtle reference to a large kitchen, while continuing on with the sophisticated market image that ties all the concepts together." The kitchen reinforces the local and home-cooked quality of the foods offered.

Kitchen cabinet styled wall fixtures sit atop a large checkerboard patterned floor and also with reference to the kitchen imagery, there is a lazy-susan used for the micro-brewery products and a cutlery or flatware stencilled design runs along the cabinets cornice. Pantry style fixtures are used along the glass walls.

"The natural maple finish contributes greatly to the image and appeal of the food products." Products such as coffee, tea, preserves, breads, candies, wines, etc. are "visually articulated to communicate more effectively to the international traveler, while adding to the character, experience and casual elegance of the space." A special graphics program was also developed for the marketplace.

The 920 sq. ft. Liar's Seafood shop was developed as "a fresh fish market with a whimsical character." The name comes from the tall tales fisherman usually tell about the "ones that got away."

A boat bottom seems to be coming down from the ceiling and the idea here was to make the customer feel as though he/she was underwater.

Fish door pulls "float" in the frameless glass doors and colorful, hand-painted wall tiles feature fish caricatures. Wharf-like merchandising displayers are casually set out on the floor and smaller cans and jars are shown on unusual, boat-shaped, glass shelving. The overall space is clean and contemporary in feeling with white tiled walls and black and white patterned mosaic tiled floors—and an abundance of light. The fresh fish is presented on beds of crushed ice in large, frameless glass showcases which are the focal point of the store's layout.

LIVERPOOL DELICATESSEN

SANTA FE, MEXICO CITY, MEXICO

The Liverpool department store is an anchor in the new 16-acre Santa Fe development in the outskirts of Mexico City. The four level store caters to young affluent families that now reside in this upscaled suburb.

The designers, Schafer Associates, used "light colored woods to suggest 'quality' to these sophisticated and brand conscious consumers" along with different ceiling heights and cove lighting to interrupt the overall sweep of the ceilings.

The delicatessen area in the new store is sleek, contemporary and as sophisticated as the rest of the store. There are almost no cliches used that one associates with food and deli except for the dried meats sus-

pended from the stainless steel grid that follows the outline of the counter below with its chamfered corners.

The area is almost all white and it is accented with a fresh, gray-green color around the counter and the canopy over the counter. The lowered ceiling carries a plentitude of soft, incandescent lamps that wash over the foods displayed in the angled glass counters and the balance of the space is subtly illuminated by the reflected light from the cove lights and some recessed fluorescents.

The designers used natural wood and recessed display alcoves, self illuminated and lined with the greenish ceramic tiles, to show off the wines and liquors along and on the rear wall of the space.

DESIGN: *Schafer Associates, Oakbrook Terrace, IL*

MARSHALL FIELD MARKETPLACE

HAWTHORNE CENTER, ILLINOIS

When Schafer Associates of Oakbrook Terrace renovated the Hawthorne Center Marshall Field store, the basement level Marketplace was also brought up to date for the new customer.

The floor in this area is covered with small white ceramic tiles and the walls are also almost stark white. Natural light colored woods are the main accents along with rustic wicker and rattan baskets. Though the space is clean, contemporary and "cool," it is warmed up by the wood and wicker and the large white glass pendant lamps that hang down over the coffee bar seen in the rear. Up front is a display

of wines on a provincial pine table and bottled gourmet gift suggestions are presented on a brass and white laminated free-standing floor fixture.

To counteract the "antique" and country style accents and accessories such as the black iron and brass baker's rack, the wooden "ice chest," the footed glass cake stands and the jig-saw cut out shelf units, the designers added the back-lit photo transparencies over the bar and the bands of blue neon that "streamline" their way around the space as a decorative frieze.

SWEETY'S CANDIES

CENTURY CITY, LOS ANGELES, CALIFORNIA

Paramount to the success of Sweety's in the Century City S/C in Los Angeles, was overcoming its location in a 400 sq. ft. space (13 ft. x 30 ft.) along a secondary corridor of shopfronts leading to one of the center's anchor department stores. The stipulation from the client was that the design be "nothing less than stunningly dramatic."

What Michael Bolton and his group designed is an "eye-opening, traffic-stopping, fantasy interplay of candy and architecture."

The shopper is immediately snared by a dazzling rainbow of over 200 imported and domestic candies brilliantly displayed in custom fabricated clear acrylic bins and illuminated with recessed fluorescent fixtures which are integrated into the "puffy white cloud" soffits and the ceiling. To add an extra dimension to the ceiling, the soffit clouds are highlighted with cove lighting. Adjustable downlights are used to accentuate the counters and the special merchandise alcoves on the walls.

As the shopper enters into the space, he/she steps on the gold "Romanesque" sun pattern on the floor which is made of ceramic tiles and extends into the balance of the shop's space. All together the design elements "reinforce and restate the atmosphere of fantasy and delight" that is associated with candy—and candy is Sweety's.

DESIGN: *Bolton Design Group, Monterey, CA*

INDEX OF STORES